'Whether we like it or not we navigate relationships every day. If you are a practitioner (e.g. counsellor, psychotherapist, coach, or use counselling skills in your work) or a trainer this is the book for you! There are a number of books on ethics. You might already be an expert on ethics. However, this book goes well beyond codes of ethics and ethical frameworks. Lynne Gabriel and Andrew Reeves invite us to consider day to day dilemmas and navigate us through the reality of relational ethics in practice. The book starts with an in-depth theory chapter and continues with a multi-voiced chapter (this I found genius) on relational ethics. Therapists and ethicists discuss relational ethics in their lived experience. The authors present quotes from the key themes discussed (following a thematic analysis). There is immediacy and creativity! Throughout the book there are examples of ethical dilemmas negotiated within relationships. Hugely helpful is the toolkit chapter where practitioners are provided with tools on how to integrate relational ethics in their work. I have enjoyed reading the chapter on pluralistic prism on relational ethics; it invites the reader to consider cultural, social, and political aspects of therapy. At the heart of navigating relational ethics is the relationship. While reading this book I realised that in my non-professional day-to-day life (e.g. family, friends, neighbours) I am confronted with ethical decision making. Knowing what's wrong and right is not enough in resolving dilemmas. The book offered me a sense of grounding and a confidence in negotiating decisions.'

Sophia Balamoutsou, PhD, *Institution for Counselling & Psychological Studies, Greece*

'This excellent book breaks new ground in understanding and applying ethical thinking in counselling and psychotherapy and provides an essential companion for anyone engaging in therapeutic practice. Gabriel and Reeves have articulated, in an accessible and directly applicable manner, the underlying philosophical understandings and plurality of ways in which ethics functions in relation to others and in context. By acknowledging the needs of practitioners working within our contemporary and multi-cultural society and the imperative to undertake fluid decision-making, this book provides the reader with confidence to navigate the hierarchies of ethical working and the uncertainties this can present, using relational ethics to guide "thinking, doing, and being" in action. I wholeheartedly recommend it to anyone in the field, from trainee to seasoned practitioner and for those who seek to work with and understand our profession.'

Kate Smith, *Professor, Head of Department of Counselling, Well-being, and Educational Psychology, University of Aberdeen, UK*

'*Navigating Relational Ethics in Day-to-Day Practice* by Gabriel and Reeves addresses a really important issue for the field, namely the gap between the ethical guidelines developed by professional bodies and knowing what the "right" thing is to do in actual practice contexts. The authors' answer, as argued across this book, is for therapy practitioners to understand that ethics must not be approached as a bureaucratic, risk management process but as a relational, embodied, lived practice that encompasses not only the work but the practitioner themselves, including their approach to doing counselling (e.g. theoretical assumptions and modality), their personal values (and biases), and their reflexivity: "we are ethics" as the final chapter concludes. Relational ethics though necessarily encompasses not just the practitioner, but also the client – and for every therapeutic context in which an ethical issue arises, the relational context includes not only the client-counsellor relationship, but also the web of relationships that both people have outside the counselling rooms – with family, friends, community, and broader society. This means, stress Gabriel and Reeves, acknowledging that relational ethics requires attention to social and political context, in particular the impacts of social injustice and inequity, and the ethical imperatives of inclusivity and decolonising practice, as well as a questioning/critical perspective on "traditional" counselling theory and practice, including approaches to ethics, on the basis that they may be exclusionary or biased. It also means that the process of ethical decision-making within relational ethics practice is necessarily both relational and collaborative, involving the counsellor engaging in transparent discussion about potential ethical issues with their clients and supporting clients to unpack the implications of different decisions. Through case studies, the authors illustrate how collaborative ethical decision-making empowers counsellors and psychotherapists and helps therapeutic dyads to arrive at decisions that "work" better for clients. The case studies are critical in supporting readers to understand practically how to integrate relational ethics into their work; additionally the book offers a "toolkit" to support relational ethical decision making in practice as well as lots of pauses for reflection that foster the reflexivity (e.g. attention to one's own biases) that is critical for relational ethics. As such, the book offers an inspiring and practical resource for the profession, trainers, and trainees. Moreover, it is only the first book in a planned series on relational ethics – I look forward to the remainder!'

Naomi Moller, *Professor, Open University, Chair of UK Training and Research Counselling Clinic Consortium (TRaCCs)*

'As its name suggests, *Navigating Relational Ethics in Day-to-Day Practice* provides pragmatic practical guidance on everyday ethical issues encountered during the practice of counselling. At the same time, the authors provide a nuanced discussion of the historical, sociological and philosophical underpinnings of a contemporary relational approach to ethics. Of particular significance, this includes challenging dominant Western discourses through adopting a pluralistic, multifaceted lens to ethics. This makes the book an invaluable resource for both students and more experienced practitioners alike, especially in grappling with complex ethical considerations around cultural diversity, colonisation, and inequities of power. Here it succeeds in being a positively radical contribution to the field.'

Brian Rodgers, PhD, *School of Counselling, Human Services & Social Work, Te Kura Tauwhiro Tangata, The University of Auckland, Waipapa Taumata Rau*

'Lynne Gabriel and Andrew Reeves offer this innovative and important compendium of contemporary perspectives on relational ethics in day-to-day practice. In so doing they have produced a core text to facilitate development of essential ethical literacy in the counselling and mental health professionals. This book will equip trainees and practitioners committed to ethical practice and development with the knowledge and skills required to navigate practice in their different professional contexts.'

Divine Charura, *Professor, Programme Director, Counselling Psychology Doctorate, York St John University, York, UK*

Navigating Relational Ethics in Day-to-Day Practice

The first in a new series on ethics in the counselling professions, *Navigating Relational Ethics in Day-to-Day Practice* contextualises the series and provides a practical 'how to' guide for bringing the theoretical concepts of ethics into practice.

Lynne Gabriel and Andrew Reeves provide a compelling explanatory narrative on the importance of translating ethical concepts into meaningful pragmatic practice and practitioner tools. They set out key theories, concepts, and contemporary challenges in practice ethics, offering multiple lenses through which to make meaning of complex practice or risk scenarios and settings. Importantly, the book considers contemporary concepts associated with social justice including working in anti-oppressive ways. The chapters feature an array of engaging material, including a round table dialogue on working ethically in day-to-day practice, a 'toolkit' for working ethically across multiple contexts and presenting issues, and a rich collection of case examples from the authors' lived experience.

This text supports trainees and practitioners in taking ethical frameworks into their direct work with clients and in their wider role in practice.

Lynne Gabriel is a British Association for Counselling and Psychotherapy (BACP) Accredited and Registered Counsellor and Psychotherapist. She is Founder-Director of the York St John University Communities Centre and founder of the associated Training, Research and Counselling Clinic Consortium (TRaCCs). In 2023, Lynne was appointed President of BACP.

Andrew Reeves is a BACP Senior Accredited Counsellor/Psychotherapist and an EMCC Senior Accredited Coach and Coach Supervisor. He has worked as a practitioner for nearly 40 years in a full range of working settings, including adult mental health crisis intervention. His research area is working with risk in the helping professions, and he has published widely in this area.

Ethics in Action
Innovative Approaches to Ethics in the Counselling Professions

Series editors

Professor Lynne Gabriel and Professor Andrew Reeves

Series description

Ethical relating and working are at the core of the counselling professions. This series provides pragmatic resources in ethics for practitioners in the psychological professions, including counsellors, psychotherapists, counselling psychologists, practitioner trainers, supervisors, and researchers, both trainee and trained. The books feature accessible and pragmatic resources on ethics in applied practice across a range of counselling and therapeutic contexts that will assist readers in decision-making in daily practice. The series aims to support meaning-making and ethical decision-making, providing responses for practitioners to key practice questions including 'so what does this mean in practice for me, working in this context, with this client group?'

Books in series

Navigating Relational Ethics in Day-to-Day Practice
Working Ethically in the Counselling Professions
Lynne Gabriel and Andrew Reeves

Navigating Relational Ethics in Day-to-Day Practice

Working Ethically in the Counselling Professions

Lynne Gabriel and
Andrew Reeves

Routledge
Taylor & Francis Group

LONDON AND NEW YORK

Designed cover image: © Getty Images

First published 2025
by Routledge
4 Park Square, Milton Park, Abingdon, Oxon OX14 4RN

and by Routledge
605 Third Avenue, New York, NY 10158

Routledge is an imprint of the Taylor & Francis Group, an informa business

© 2025 Lynne Gabriel and Andrew Reeves

The right of Lynne Gabriel and Andrew Reeves to be
identified as authors of this work has been asserted in
accordance with sections 77 and 78 of the Copyright,
Designs and Patents Act 1988.

British Library Cataloguing-in-Publication Data
A catalogue record for this book is available from the British Library

Library of Congress Cataloging-in-Publication Data
Names: Gabriel, Lynne, author. | Reeves, Andrew
(Counsellor), author.
Title: Navigating relational ethics in day-to-day practice :
working ethically in the counselling professions / Lynne
Gabriel and Andrew Reeves.
Identifiers: LCCN 2024016968 (print) | LCCN 2024016969 (ebook) |
ISBN 9781032408507 (hardback) | ISBN 9781032408491 (paperback) |
ISBN 9781003354970 (ebook)
Subjects: LCSH: Counselors—Professional ethics. | Counseling—
Moral and ethical aspects. | Counseling—Vocational guidance.
Classification: LCC BF636.67 .G33 2025 (print) |
LCC BF636.67 (ebook) | DDC 174/.91583—dc23/eng/20240603
LC record available at https://lccn.loc.gov/2024016968
LC ebook record available at https://lccn.loc.gov/2024016969

ISBN: 9781032408507 (hbk)
ISBN: 9781032408491 (pbk)
ISBN: 9781003354970 (ebk)

DOI: 10.4324/9781003354970

Typeset in Times New Roman
by codeMantra

Dedication

I have been fortunate to encounter some precious people in my life – not least my wife Patti and my cherished friends and colleagues. Love, compassion, care, congruence, challenge, and inspiration. Thank you for your relational gifts and for contributing to a life worth living.

Lynne Gabriel

At the core of this text is the value and importance of relationships. I would like to dedicate this book to Diane, Adam, Katie, and Emily and all my friends and colleagues who have taught me about living a good life.

Andrew Reeves

Contents

Acknowledgements

Working with Andrew has been a joy. Journeying to the point in time where Routledge offered us the contract to deliver a series on *Ethics in Action*, then onwards to now, and to the publication of our introductory book, has been an absolute pleasure in Andrew's company!

Ethics has been part of the warp and weft of my life, weaving a way through all my work in counselling and mental health. Navigating those decades led to multiple attempts to chart ethical routes through complex human relationships, meaning making and ways of working. Earlier publications and professional work reflect this, including earlier textbooks and papers that explore or touch on relational ethics. It has been deeply rewarding to develop relational ethics in contemporary counselling and its wider contexts through research conversations with the contributors to Chapter 2. A huge 'thank you' to those who contributed their experiences and wisdom to Chapter 2. Alistair Ross, Dwight Turner, Gillian Proctor, Hadyn Williams, John Wilson, Linda Finlay, Myira Khan, Peter Blundell, and Rich Knight – you are incredible people. Your voices are wonderfully rich, evoking the complexities and challenges of navigating human relationships and relational ethics. Your contributions bring a compassionate core and heart to the book.

Andrew has highlighted below our great Routledge commissioning editor, Grace, and editorial assistant, Sarah, and their colleagues who supported production. Thank you all for your work and support. Also highlighted below are many friends, colleagues, peer reviewers and series authors who have inspired, and brought their unique presences and influences to bear on the processes of generating ideas and building textbook narratives. Being involved in the pluralistic practice community felt like I had found my tribe. From the incredible forces of nature, John McLeod and Mick Cooper, through to brilliant rising talent like Christine Kupfer and Nicola Blunden, you are truly amazing. Finally, John Wilson and Rachel Wicaksono at York St John have been fundamental to my life in recent years; thank you for your precious and much appreciated support.

Lynne Gabriel

Sometimes you can be sitting quietly minding your own business and something wonderful lands in your lap; or your inbox, which feels like a modern-day virtual lap. I received an email from Lynne Gabriel with the germ of an idea: how about a new series of books on ethics that would be accessible, relevant, and speak directly to the heart of practice, and would I be interested in joining her on this journey as co-author and co-Series Editor? Would I be interested? In truth, I had to ponder this a little before replying, so six seconds later my reply email was winging its way back to Lynne with a hearty, 'yes please'. What a superb idea and my first acknowledgement, therefore, is to Lynne for this wonderful opportunity.

As a practitioner of over 35 years standing, ethics has been the golden thread, always evident in my thinking, learning and doing. Sometimes ethics has felt impenetrable to me: a set of abstract philosophical ideas that, in truth, has sometimes been hard to weave into my work, to inform the relationship I had with clients, colleagues, peers and, indeed, friends and family. This book and the other books in this series, have been shaped by the wisdom and insights of others, with a primary aim of being accessible to all, for which I am hugely grateful. Additionally, and particularly for Chapter 2, those wonderful people who gave freely of their time to meet and talk with us about their own perspectives and experiences about ethics; both Lynne and I learnt so much and we are hugely grateful to them.

To Grace McDonnell and Sarah Hafeez at Routledge, who championed this idea from its conception, as well as the many others at Routledge who have worked hard behind the scenes to bring it to fruition. Finally, to the peer reviewers, many colleagues and friends who have inspired with their insight and enlivened with their humour, particularly everyone in the Pluralistic Practice community (www.pluralisticpractice.com), with a specific shout out to John McLeod, Julia McLeod, Nicola Blunden, Sophia Balamoutsou, Mhairi Thurston,

Caryl Sibbett, Caz Binstead, Nicholas Sarantakis, Kirsten Amis, Jane Darougar, Windy Dryden, Kate Smith, John Wilson (Online Events), John Wilson (York St John), Mick Cooper, Brian Rodgers, Divine Charura, and Naomi Moller. Thank you all.

Andrew Reeves

Foreword

We have both been practitioners and trainers for many years, so have encountered ethics in multiple ways at many points in our working lives. When looking at other, allied professions to counselling and psychotherapy – and across other disciplines too, such as law – ethics is the bedrock to what is widely considered good practice. We have learnt, however, that ethics means different things to different people: for some, ethics is about curiosity, uncertainty, and the changing dynamic of our therapeutic world; for others, it can feel at worst incomprehensible or impenetrable and thus, irrelevant to practice or, at best, simply a set of 'rights' and 'wrongs' to be followed.

We look for certainty because we need to find a solution to a particular problem, only to encounter what feels like a hall of mirrors reflecting umpteen possibilities. The danger is that we perceive ethics to speak of binary positions: of 'rights' and 'wrongs', of 'good' and 'bad', with little to say for the grey areas of our work. Whereas in fact, ethics allows us to begin to find our way of navigating the grey areas, where we can reach some deeper understanding and embark on a road with some clearer rationale and confidence in what we do.

Lynne had the idea for a series of books that spoke to various aspects of practice, but in a way that helped practitioners think about their own relationship with ethics so that ethical engagement could become embedded in day-to-day work. But more than that: to think about ethics as a relational process, for that is what the core of our work is built on – relationships. One of the struggles we have as practitioners is seeing ethics as sitting *outside* of our work, which we turn to at time of difficulty. Whereas the premise here is that ethics sit *within* our work, present in every moment, all the time. This includes when client(s) are sitting in our room, or online, or at the end of an email, or before they first connect with us, and after they have left us. Ethics is about our 'being' as practitioners: in our training, learning, continuing professional development, supervision, with peers, colleagues, other disciplines, in our online social media activities and, well, in everything we do and who we are.

In writing this introductory text to the series we spoke with many to bring as diverse a perspective as possible. We are hugely grateful to those who gave their time to be interviewed by us, and who form the co-authors of Chapter 2: Alistair Ross, Dwight Turner, Gillian Proctor, Hadyn Williams, John Wilson, Linda Finlay, Myira Khan, Peter Blundell and Rich Knight. Your individual and combined wisdom left us excited, inspired and a little wiser and we are eternally grateful for it.

We are so fortunate too to have other amazing authors in our series, including John McLeod and Julia McLeod (who have written on participatory ethics in pluralistic research); Caz Binstead and Nicholas Sarantakis (who have written about ethics in private practice); and Nicola Blunden and Mhairi Thurston (who have written about navigating ethical partnerships). We have future books planned too, including on single-session therapy and ethics in education settings.

Fundamentally, we hope this book – which introduces the concept of navigating relational ethics in day-to-day practice – and the wider series, helps bridge some of the gaps that can sometimes sit between practitioners and ways of working with ethics. We hope you find this book engaging and accessible, and that it prompts thinking and reflection to further support your own practice; it has done that for us.

Professor Lynne Gabriel, York
Professor Andrew Reeves, Chester

Chapter 1

Navigating relational ethics in day-to-day practice

Introduction

In *Navigating Ethics in Day-to-Day Practice*, as the *Ethics in Action* series editors, we provide an explanatory narrative on the translation of philosophical, cultural, social, and ethical concepts into meaningful and pragmatic tools for practitioners in their day-to-day practice. As editors we are both active in the helping professions and have published and consulted within the areas of training, research, practice, and professional practice and research ethics. We are committed to advancing concepts and practices to provide information, knowledge, and lived-life experiences that capture contemporary challenges and contexts within the counselling and therapy professions. We draw from rich, multiple knowledge and meaning-making sources including history, sociology, philosophy, human geography, and organisational and systems psychology, to inform the narratives of this and subsequent chapters.

We consider ways in which traditional codes of ethics within helping professions are principle-based and rooted in medicalised and Euro-centric theory and concepts. On the contrary, contemporary practice and helping relationships demand more fluid and reflexive approaches that can be informed by virtues, values, professional heritage, social justice, and an understanding and acknowledgement of societal and cultural injustices. Developments in deconstructing colonisation within the counselling professions (see for example, Turner, 2021 and 2023) provide a rich contemporary context and backdrop through which to develop and extend how we move forward with the supporting framework that relational ethics can provide. We posit meaning-making and ethical decision-making as accessible, pragmatic, and dynamic practitioner tools and competencies that offer a departure point for ethics in action. We offer definitions of key terms used in the book, offer brief descriptions of the remaining chapters, and conclude

DOI: 10.4324/9781003354970-1

with an overview of the book collection that will launch our *Ethics in Action* series. These are all signposted by the ever-present question for us as authors: 'so what does this mean in practice, for me, for my work in this particular context, with this client group, or this client?'

In working with diverse and multidimensional issues and challenges, counselling and mental health professionals frequently engage with risk and risky situations. Risk is an inherent dimension of work in the human helping and mental health professions. We are all exposed to risk. It is ever-present and we cannot 'edit it out'. Developing *risk resilience* through personal and professional experiences and developmental activities can support practitioners to sustain themselves – and their clients – through the inevitable day-to-day challenges. Working with diversity and risk necessitates practitioner reflexivity and capacity for emotionally informed empathy (Jolly, 2022).

In the following sections we present heritage concepts that underpin today's practice ethics within the counselling professions. We provide a definition and description of *relational ethics*. We offer a brief consideration of virtues, values, and principles-based ethics, in recognition of philosophical and relational values of care, compassion, and empathy that are associated with developing a *pluralistic mindset* for ethics in practice. Epistemic justice and the importance of authentically valuing and actively collaborating with clients as they journey to chart, construct, and reconstruct their experiences, perceptions, and hopes, features here. We then go on to reflect on the complex cultural, social, and political features of justice in relation to meaning-making and decision-making. These concepts, and those considered below, are woven throughout subsequent chapters and the textbooks in the *Ethics in Action* series.

Principles, virtues, and values: what are they and what do they mean for practice ethics?

A principles-based approach is rooted in philosophical premises that support humans to *do the right thing*. Dominant within medical and social care health settings, organising principles include autonomy (respecting clients' rights for informed consent), beneficence (acting in the client's best interests), and non-maleficence (doing no harm to clients) (Beauchamp and Childress, 2019). A principles-based approach is informed by codes of conduct and ethical frameworks that set out essential principles and associated practice rules or duties.

Most codes provided by professional bodies and associations indicate the behavioural consequences of unethical behaviour. Codes, when contravened, also provide context for professional conduct complaints cases. Whilst principles and derived codes offer tools to inform decisions and meaning-making in action, perceptions about their dogmatic status can negatively influence practitioners' abilities to reflexively apply the principles in practice.

Central to virtue ethics are two key concepts – *human virtues* and *practical wisdom*. Essentially, this refers to character traits (virtues) and dispositions (practical understandings, innate or learned wisdom, ideals) that positively influence their possessors' beliefs, perceptions, and behaviours. Virtues are aspirational and can interact pragmatically and positively with humans' abilities and tendencies for practical wisdom. Additionally, they are historically, culturally, and socially located. Since Ancient Greece, multiple philosophers and theorists have considered human virtues. In the 1800s they informed the development of medical ethics and, more recently, they underpinned Seligman's innovation of positive psychology (Seligman, 2011) and Goleman's conception of emotional intelligence (Goleman, 2005). Essentially, contemporary approaches that consider virtue ethics will co-opt dominant values to inform meaning-making and decision-making in practice. The virtues and practical wisdom of the person or people involved in the meaning-making and decision-making will also inform their *intentionality* both within their counselling and mental health work and through into the wider context of the helping professions and beyond.

Typically, the concept of values is used to convey human behaviours informed by lived-life experiences and perceptions. From a practice ethics perspective, key values common to humans include 'do no harm' to our clients. Values also form part of our collective or creative consciousness and inform how we practise both within the counselling professions and throughout our lives and relationships. The philosophical concept of 'value pluralism' was popularised by Isaiah Berlin, a 20th-century Russian-British philosopher, whose ideas informed political and sociological theories. Berlin's ideas continue to be relevant in the complex and conflicted contemporary global landscape. Berlin believed that it was impossible to reconcile irreconcilable humanity. Instead, we need to acknowledge diversity of belief and opinion and identify humane and diverse ways of co-existing; ways that avoid violence and exploitation (Berlin, 2013). Human values inform a value pluralism approach to ethics and here we use the term *pluralistic mindset* and adopt aspects of pluralistic thinking and practices to inform ways forward for contemporary ethics. This perspective is consistent with a pluralistic approach to therapy (Cooper & McLeod, 2011).

Unsurprisingly, principles and virtues are similar concepts that describe features of being human. When we factor in values, we can see how all three are intricately linked, essentially providing contributory elements for ethics in lived contexts. Whilst principles provide the basis for codes and promote global practices in relation to the provision of care, virtues are rooted in people's and communities' narratives and aspirations (Meara et al. 1996), thereby bringing opportunities to consider practice through nuanced multicultural and multidimensional lenses. Viewed through a pluralistic mindset, the choiceful and intentional use of relevant principles, virtues, and values offers a means through which to better inform our decision-making and helping work.

Relational ethics – what are they?

We both bring professional and personal curiosities to conceptualising and practising *relational ethics*. The concept of *relational ethics* for the counselling professions originates from the work of Gabriel and Casemore (2009), Gabriel (2005), and from educational and care philosophy developed by Nell Noddings (2013). It is informed by Emmanuel Levinas' ideas on phenomenology and active interest in people's lived experiences and perceptions. Building on Levinas and Noddings' ideas about human relationships, and Goffman's (1971) ideas about relational roles and interactions, Gabriel and Casemore (2009) conceived relational ethics in counselling and psychotherapy as complex dimensions through which the nature and progress of a helping relationship are mindfully and ethically engaged with.

Here, we extend Gabriel and Casemore's definition and overtly encompass justice, anti-oppressive practice, epistemic trust, and inclusivity. We bring a pluralistic mindset to ethics in action, and define a pluralistic relational ethics as an approach that

> acknowledges complex relational and liminal processes through which decisions, nuanced interactions, and meaning making associated with helping relationships and work are mindfully and reflexively engaged with. **Pluralistic relational ethics** afford authentic compassionate attention to social, cultural, racial, and

political dimensions, as well as to inclusivity, anti-oppression, collaboration, and recognition of the positive impact, contributions, and implications of diverse relational concepts and contexts.

Contemporary developments in relational ethics embed ethics of care and compassion (Gabriel & Casemore, 2009; Finlay, 2019; Noddings, 2013). This is not care within the context of a medicalised notion of mental and emotional wellbeing. It is not a health service approach that pathologises, individualises, and problematises people's mental health. Rather, it acknowledges the centrality of relationships (whether dyadic, group, community, organisation, or global communities), works with participant power in relationships, mitigates against oppression, and adopts de-pathologising dynamics.

Essential to the ongoing development of relational ethics is a mindset that recognises the value of a pluralistic *ever evolving iterative and deliberate approach* to practice ethics. Such a pluralistic mindset and approach acknowledges the existence of unknown underlying forces and accepts the conflicted nature of human existence. It also recognises emergent pragmatic and theoretical transitions in practitioners' attempts to navigate through chaotic, conflicted, and nuanced human experiences, perceptions, beliefs, and behaviours. This approach, or mindset, requires recognition of inherent relational processes and decision-making that are complex, iterative, and reflexive. Such questing is part of being human, within a human relations profession, and involves the pragmatics and practicalities of meaning-making and decision-making in practice. It also acknowledges the impact of the wider social, cultural, and political domains. Relational ethics acknowledges the discursive and dialectical dimensions of human interactions and communications, and of being in relationship with others.

Relational ethics requires cultural competence and awareness of ethnic, cultural, social, and political complexities. For example, African and Asian moral philosophies tend to place familial and relational bonds at the core of life and living. This has significant implications for helping theories and practices which are predominantly rooted in colonialised, Western, white, middle-class, predominantly male, individualised, and privileged perspectives. Practitioners need to transition to conceptualisations and pragmatic practices that are culturally and socially sensitive. Gabriel (2005) articulated a way of perceiving and considering relational dynamics and ethics, using the concept of

Figure 1.1 A relational ethics orrery

the 'orrery' (a Victorian concept, which displayed the orbiting and interacting planets in the then-known galaxy) to depict a fluid and interactional process. See Figure 1.1 for an outline of Gabriel's original interactive concept of relational ethics. This concept is explored in more detail in Gabriel and Casemore 2009. It is explored here in Chapter 4, where we extend the concept to develop pluralistic relational ethics, then again in Chapters 6 and 7.

Social, cultural, and political epistemic justice – what does this mean?

Epistemic injustice is a concept developed by British philosopher Miranda Fricker (Fricker, 2009). Essentially, Fricker saw that people could be wronged, specifically in their capacity as a knower, or a person with lived experience of being in a helping relationship, or someone being supported in the context of a group or system. Existing concepts can further inform how we interpret injustices and the toxic 'othering' of fellow humans. For Edith Stein (Monjaraz Fuentes, 2022), a German Jewish feminist philosopher and nun, our openness to a synthesis between '*I*' and '*Other*' could generate authentic community and connectivity; a position that resonates with a pluralistic ethics mindset, which accepts difference and diversity, and seeks genuine, meaningful interactions and connections.

Recognition of dynamic interaction and a capacity to move between inner and outer contexts is grounded in a belief that humans can make choices and act intentionally, whilst embedding those choices and intentions in the values of empathy and care. According to Hanlon (2022) *relational justice* values interdependence over independence, in the recognition that human existence involves interconnected individuals, groups and systems of care and emotional capital. Interdependence at community, national, and international levels is in constant flux. The impact of climate change, international conflict, and global pandemics will accompany clients into any helping that they access. The national, international, and global inequities that exist, including poverty, discrimination, human trafficking, exploitation, and abuse will feature in some of the client stories heard by therapists. There are implications for care of clients, as well as self-care/other-care and compassion. Increasingly the helping professions are involved in political and international landscapes in their quests for global compassion, collaboration, and growth of co-production in mental health development, delivery, and research (Groot et al. 2022).

Innovation in relational ethics concepts and practices is most evident in recent pluralistic work (Smith et al., 2021). However, it is important to acknowledge that novel approaches usually reconfigure or co-opt historical ideas. One such idea, the original legal concept of *fiduciary,* is co-opted within the context of helping work and denotes the provision of services that epitomise loyalty, faithfulness, confidentiality, and trustworthiness. Fiduciary is co-opted into codes of ethics in the form of the virtue 'fidelity'. Seen through a relational ethics lens, it conveys the building of faith and trust in relationships, and in the contexts of groups, systems, communities, or societies, it infers interconnectedness, interdependence, and the power of living compassionately and reflexively, rather than defensively through dissent and conflict.

Adopting a fiduciary approach is both process-oriented and iterative and is consistent with an open and emergent relational ontology, or way of being (Mussel, 2022). Navigating relationships in the spirit of trust, faith, awareness, and competence, to support transition through the liminal relational dynamics inherent in the helping professions, resonates with an *ethic of care* (Finlay, 2019; Gabriel, 2005; Noddings, 2013). In the context of contemporary human and societal challenges, there is a pressing need to work with pluralistic relational ethics to generate situated and relational meaning-making. In a post-pandemic world, we can draw upon relational (fiduciary) values and virtues to inform our ethical reasoning and to generate a facilitative approach to relational ethics (Mifsud & Herlihy, 2022). Essentially, we can quest and craft ways of being, behaving and living with and through the contextualised prisms of a pluralistic mindset. Through creative dialogical and discursive approaches and processes, the building blocks for pluralistic relational ethics for the counselling and mental health professions are present.

Introduction to subsequent chapters

Chapter 1: Introducing the Ethics in Action series

The authors provide a compelling explanatory narrative on the importance of translating ethical concepts into meaningful pragmatic practice and practitioner tools. The chapter will note key principles informing the text. It posits meaning-making and ethical decision-making as accessible practitioner tools and competencies and offers a departure point, signposted by the question: 'So what does this mean in practice for me, working in this context, with this client group?' The chapter concludes with brief descriptions of the series editions.

Chapter 2: Experiences of ethics in practice

This chapter presents contributions from the authors and published authors in the field of practice ethics (including Alistair Ross, Dwight Turner, Gillian Proctor, Hadyn Williams, John Wilson, Linda Finlay, Myira Khan, Peter Blundell, Rich Knight). Discussions were prompted through the following questions:

- What are the key ethical challenges facing the psychological professions and their practitioners and clients?

- What historical and contemporary theory, concepts, practices, and 'received wisdom' support you in working ethically?
- What is missing from extant ethics guides and publications?

From the discussions, we identify key themes and foreground these as important factors when considering cutting-edge relational ethics for the counselling professions. These themes will be represented in this textbook, as well as be visible in other titles in the series.

Chapter 3: Thinking about ethics in practice

This chapter sets out key theories, concepts, and contemporary challenges in practice ethics. It offers multiple pragmatic lenses through which to make meaning of complex practice or risk scenarios and settings. The chapter engages with the complexities of ethical codes, frameworks, and theories, whilst capturing the challenges and reality of day-to-day meaning-making, decision-making, and associated practices. In essence, outlining practice examples of how we translate information for ethical codes and frameworks into our day-to-day work as practitioners.

Chapter 4: Reflexive ethical practice

This chapter provides tangible and pragmatic resources for navigating ethics in day-to-day practice across a range of contexts. It additionally considers how practitioners can build in reflective ethical engagement in their day-to-day work, building their own experiential benchmarking process to support ongoing practice while, at the same time, embedding ethical thinking into their professional reflexivity.

Chapter 5: Building an ethics in action toolkit

The authors present a pluralistic, relational approach to ethics in action. Drawing upon exemplar approaches to ethics, latest research (findings from focus groups) and informed by pluralistic values and concepts, a 'toolkit' for working ethically across multiple contexts and presenting issues is offered, including how such a 'toolkit' might be translated into a multidisciplinary context, as well as adapted for other allied professionals.

Chapter 6: Case studies

This chapter creatively engages with case examples from lived experience and draws from the ethics in action toolkit and resources provided in Chapters 4 and 5 to support meaning-making and decision-making, ultimately offering a rich array of cases. The cases provide valuable resources for trainers, supervisors, service leads, practitioners, and trainees and anyone interested in exploring in-depth material on work in the counselling professions.

Chapter 7: Integrating ethics within and across boundaries

The final chapter summarises key themes from the book and posits a pluralistic prism for practice ethics, providing key signposting for the counselling professions, while also being relevant to readers who work across allied professions. The chapter responds to the key themes derived from our research contributors in Chapter 2.

Introduction to textbooks included in the launch of the initial series and their planned titles

Ethically Informed Therapy Training, by **Julia McLeod, Lynne Thomas, and John McLeod**: Counselling and psychotherapy training comprises a complex and challenging learning arena for both students and their tutors. Within a therapy training course, a student is expected to reflect on, share, and critically engage with potentially sensitive areas of personal experience, while at the same time developing skills and competencies associated with a capacity to work in a largely autonomous manner with deeply troubled individuals, families, and groups. Students in a programme are typically encouraged to provide supportive and constructive feedback to each other, participate as members of a learning community, and act in client roles for colleagues practising counselling skills and intervention. Tutors on therapy training programmes need to be able to maintain a safe space within which emotional and interpersonal learning can take place, alongside fulfilling the requirements of their college, institute or university, the professional body accrediting the programme, and local stakeholders such as placement agencies. Both the personal learning undertaken by students, and the professional skills being developed, are inevitably permeated by ethical issues existing within the wider society, such as deep inequalities and injustices experienced by marginalised groups.

The aim of the present book is to highlight the ethical challenges and opportunities associated with training in counselling and psychotherapy, in relation to the experience and perspective of both tutors/trainers and students/trainees. The book begins by succinctly summarising ethical concepts and strategies, such as informed consent, confidentiality and avoidance of harm, and social justice values, that form the foundations of the prevailing consensus around ethically-sound educational practice, and how these principles have been understood and implemented by professional bodies in the therapy field. This is followed by a series of chapters that address specific ethical issues associated with therapy training. The closing chapter looks at how explicit attention during training to ethical reflexivity, and facilitation of dialogue around ethical challenges arising within the training setting, can play a vital role in preparing students to learn about how to offer forms of counselling and psychotherapy that promote social justice.

Co-Producing Counselling and Psychotherapy: Navigating Ethical Partnerships in the Therapeutic Professions, by **Nicola Blunden and Mhairi Thurston**: This book provides an accessible, practical, and thorough handbook for professionals who are engaged in co-producing therapy or mental health research with clients, or who find themselves liaising with multidisciplinary teams, or who are part of a system of co-produced 'wraparound' care. The volume aims to resource practitioners and researchers with confidence and competence to navigate the choppy ethical waters of co-production, and to achieve best practice in supporting clients' welfare and flourishing.

The text provides counselling and psychotherapy professionals with an overview of co-production ethics. It proposes a model for thinking through complex co-produced ethical issues. It also provides readers with a range of illustrative examples of how professionals and lay people have together navigated ethical problems and opportunities in their work. Readers are supported throughout the text to apply the model to their own work. It also provides a co-production ethics 'lingua franca' for therapists working with allied professionals in multidisciplinary teams.

The book is aimed at trainee and qualified counselling professionals and researchers, as well as allied professionals using counselling skills in their work, and who are co-producing counselling or therapy with clients. Co-production is a growing practice within health and social care services in the U.K., emerging from a wider co-productive turn across society. In health and social care, it is related to shared decision-making and person-centred care practices. Because of the acknowledged 'messy and innovative' nature of co-production, as well as its contextual situatedness, and its nesting within multiple systems of care, ethical decision-making is necessarily complex. Further, co-produced ethical relations frequently take place in high-risk social and medical populations. There is currently no model of co-production ethics for counselling professionals, who are sometimes the central point of contact for persons receiving co-produced care.

Relational Ethics in Psychotherapy and Counselling Private Practice: Justice, Solidarity and Care, by **Caz Binstead** and **Nicholas Sarantakis**: The authors posit that the key defining element of private practice is that the practitioner does the contracting with the client (meaning they hold full responsibility and control of their practice, and relationship with their individual clients). The authors are aware of the grey areas around marketing and referrals with third parties, such as referral agencies. Indeed, collaboration with various agencies and platforms may provide different levels of responsibility and control to the associate, which may make the boundaries of private practice less clear. Therefore, this book will discuss certain aspects of such contracts with third parties and the implications for the private practitioner so that the latter can make informed judgments on whether taking up such opportunities could potentially compromise their values and ways of working.

Most private practitioners would align explicitly with a specific ethics code of their professional body and have an awareness of the importance of ethical practice. However, there is inevitably a gap between generic ethical guidelines (and other mediums, containing theoretical reflections) and hands-on private practice. In particular, ethics codes normally would want to allow some flexibility in the way private practitioners apply their guidelines, because, understandably, certain situations require an individualised approach in ethical decision-making (BACP, 2018, Introduction). This means there is more responsibility (and potentially, pressure), for the lone working private practitioner – who holds full control of their practice – in managing the task of effectively applying ethical decision-making and making sense of these gaps in practice. In addition, across the board, ethical codes may have other general limitations, or outdated information, when it comes to the 21st-century private practitioner and their all-round experience, i.e. the ethics of setting up, building, and working in their unique, individual private practices. Therefore, this book invites a much-needed open reflection with a 'bottom-up' practice-based approach (rather than suggesting 'prescriptive guidelines'). This open discussion is indeed important because a) private practitioners are working within a more isolated context anyway, and in a niche area that, as anecdotal evidence suggests, is likely to have not been adequately covered in training; b) there is a lack of organisational scaffolding when working in private practice; c) there has historically, been a lack of open (public) discussion about common ethical dilemmas that a private practitioner may come across; d) there is more chance of unintended ethical mistakes, owing to additional factors, such as running a business and how this might potentially conflict with the practice of ethical therapy.

Ethics in Participatory Research on Counselling and Psychotherapy, by John McLeod and Julia McLeod: Both as active practitioner-researchers, and as critical consumers of research, counsellors and psychotherapists are required to understand the ethical principles and procedures that constitute key aspects of the context of contemporary research practice. Increasingly, therapy practitioners and researchers position themselves within a pluralistic perspective that respects the value of multiple sources of knowledge and draws on the active participation of multiple stakeholders. The aim of the present book is to highlight the distinctive ethical challenges and opportunities associated with a pluralistic orientation to research on psychotherapy, with a particular focus on how these factors unfold in participatory research in which stakeholders (clients, service users, practitioners, members of the public) are actively involved in the research process. The book begins by succinctly summarising ethical concepts and strategies, such as informed consent, confidentiality, and avoidance of harm, that form the foundations of the prevailing consensus around ethically-sound research. An overview of distinctive ethical features of participatory research is then provided, highlighting the notion of active and intentional ethical commitment as an essential strand within this type of investigation. This is followed by a series of chapters that address specific ethics issues. The closing chapter discusses approaches to training and ethical inquiry, the establishment of communities of research practice, and the synergy between ethical reflexivity in research and the provision of forms of counselling and psychotherapy that promote social justice.

While primarily intended as a resource for researchers and research consumers in the psychological professions (counsellors, psychotherapists, counselling psychologists, practitioner trainers and supervisors, both trainee and trained), the ethical and methodological issues being discussed in this book will be explored in a way that will be relevant for students and practitioners in allied professions including social work, teaching, nursing, and the broader mental health professions. For example, several of the case examples cited in the book refer to studies whose scope is interdisciplinary and interprofessional. In addition, the book aims to be accessible and relevant to community members and organisations involved in co-produced and collaborative research studies.

Chapter conclusion

We have now set the scene for this textbook and for the initial series in which it sits, *Ethics in Action: Innovative Approaches to Ethics in the Counselling Professions.*

In the following chapter, we engage with contributions from key figures in the UK counselling professions who engaged in research conversation with us, with a view to considering the current 'state of ethics' in the counselling professions and horizon scanning to identify 'what's missing' from contemporary approaches to ethics.

References

BACP (2018). *Ethical Framework for the Counselling Professions.* BACP.

Beauchamp, T.L. & Childress, J.F. (2019). *Principles of Biomedical Ethics.* Oxford University Press.

Berlin, I. (2013). *The Crooked Timber of Humanity: Chapters in the History of Ideas* (2nd Ed). Princeton University Press.

Cooper, M. & McLeod, J. (2011). Person-centered Therapy: A Pluralistic Perspective. *Person-Centered and Experiential Psychotherapies*, 10(3), 210–223. doi:10.1080/14779757.2011.599517

Finlay, L. (2019). *Practical Ethics in Counselling and Psychotherapy: A Relational Approach.* Sage.

Fricker, M. (2009). *Epistemic Injustice: Power and the Ethics of Knowing.* Oxford University Press.

Gabriel, L. (2005). *Speaking the Unspeakable: The Ethics of Dual Relationships in Counselling and Psychotherapy.* Routledge.

Gabriel, L. & Casemore, R. (2009). Eds. *Relational Ethics in Practice: Narratives from Counselling and Psychotherapy.* Routledge.

Goffman, E. (1971). *The Presentation of Self in Everyday Life*. Penguin Books.

Goleman, D. (2005). *Emotional Intelligence*. Bantam Books.

Groot, B., Haveman, A., & Abma, T. (2022). Relational, Ethically Sound Co-production in Mental Health Care Research: Epistemic Injustice and the Need for an Ethics of Care, *Critical Public Health*, 32(2), 230–240. doi:10.1080/09581596.2020.1770694

Hanlon, N. (2022). Relational Justice and Relational Pedagogy in Professional Social Care Work, *Social Work Education*. doi:10.1080/02615479. 2022.2123913

Jolly, M. (2022). Putting the Emotion Back into Empathy: Edith Stein's Understanding of Empathy Applied to Contemporary Issues. In: Andrews, M.F., Calcagno, A. (eds) *Ethics and Metaphysics in the Philosophy of Edith Stein. Women in the History of Philosophy and Sciences*, vol 12. Springer, Cham. doi:10.1007/978-3-030–91198-0_3

Meara, N.M., Schmidt, L.D., & Day, J.D. (1996). Principles and Virtues: A foundation for ethical decisions, policies and character. *The Counseling Psychologist*. 24(1): 4–77.

Mifsud, A. & Herlihy, B. (2022) Ethical Standards for a Post-COVID-19 World. *Journal of Mental Health Counseling* 44(1): 82–96. doi:10.17744/ mehc.44.1.07

Monjaraz Fuentes, P. (2022). Ontology and Relational Ethics in Edith Stein's Thought. In: Andrews, M.F., Calcagno, A. (eds) *Ethics and Metaphysics in the Philosophy of Edith Stein. Women in the History of Philosophy and Sciences*, vol 12. Springer, Cham. doi:10.1007/978-3-030– 91198-0_15

Mussel, H.J. (2022). Theorising the Fiduciary: Ontology and Ethics. *Journal of Business Ethics*. doi:10.1007/s10551-022-05235-6

Noddings, N. (2013). *Caring: A Feminine Approach to Ethics and Moral Education: A Relational Approach to Ethics and Moral Education*. University of California Press.

Seligman, M. (2011). *Flourish: A New Understanding of Happiness and Wellbeing*. Nicholas Brealey Publishing.

Smith, K., McLeod, J., Blunden, N., Cooper, M., Gabriel, L., Kupfer, C., McLeod, J., Murphie, M-C., Oddli, H.W., Thurston, M., Winter, L.A. (2021). A Pluralistic Perspective on Research in Psychotherapy: Harnessing Passion, Difference and Dialogue to Promote Justice and Relevance. *Frontiers in Psychology*, 12. doi:10.3389/fpsyg.2021.742676

Turner, D. (2021). *Intersections of Privilege and Otherness in Counselling & Psychotherapy: Mockingbird*. Routledge.

Turner, D. (2023). *The Psychology of Supremacy: Imperium*. Routledge.

Chapter 2

Contributions from lived experience counsellors, therapists, and ethicists

Lynne Gabriel, Andrew Reeves, Alistair Ross, Dwight Turner, Gillian Proctor, Hadyn Williams, John Wilson, Linda Finlay, Myira Khan, Peter Blundell, Rich Knight

Introduction

In this chapter we present contributions from experienced authors, academics, trainers, researchers, practitioners, and activists in the counselling and mental health professions; all of them individuals who have engaged with ethical challenges and demands across diverse working contexts. Our contributors are Alistair Ross, Dwight Turner, Gillian Proctor, Hadyn Williams, John Wilson, Linda Finlay, Myira Khan, Peter Blundell, and Rich Knight. Their voices and contributions form a rich and multidimensional depiction of ethics in life and lived relationships.

We both value the contribution that evidence-based and practice-informed work and research has made to the counselling and mental health professions. It was important to us both that we created the opportunity to embed research in the textbook, whilst at the same time, craft chapter narratives that were accessible for a non-academic audience. To create the narrative for this chapter, we wanted to hear from people with life and lived experiences of navigating the ethical relationships and landscapes of counselling and helping. We adopted what researchers refer to as purposive sampling, whereby we identified, discussed, and agreed individuals in the counselling professions who we could approach and invite to contribute rich narratives on contemporary notions of ethics. Colleagues were invited to participate in an exploratory conversation and were provided with information about the purpose of the research conversations as well as with informed consent documents to inform their decision-making about

DOI: 10.4324/9781003354970-2

being involved. All contributors are trailblazers who have made significant contributions to theory, practice, and research within and beyond the counselling and helping professions.

In relation to the research processes that we followed prior to inviting people to the research conversations, there were several steps. Following conceptualisation of the book, our desire was to embed meaningful and helpful research within the textbook, so our next step was to secure ethical approval from the York St John University Cross-School Research Ethics Committee. After receipt of formal approval, we organised the research conversations, which were facilitated through recorded MS Teams video meetings. This gave us access to a video recording and a good quality audio transcription, saving considerable transcription time. A draft of the chapter was shared with contributors. Additionally, the themes and the textbook will inform an online event aimed at engaging people in accessing and authentically embedding relational ethics in practice.

In relation to how we present the richness of the colleagues' contributions, we identify the key themes and provide narrative that describes the theme, its scope and scale. Importantly, we include extracts from contributors' narratives, to bring alive the notion of authentic ethics in action.

The research conversations with colleagues were prompted through the following questions:

Box 2.1 Research conversations – key questions

1. What are the key ethical challenges facing the psychological professions and their practitioners and clients?
2. What historical and contemporary theory, concepts, practices, and wisdom support you in working ethically?
3. What is missing from extant ethics guides and publications?

Following the research conversations, we reviewed the transcripts and, informed by Braun and Clarke (2021), used a process of reflexive thematic analyses to draw out key themes related to the above areas of questioning and to the overall topic of ethics in practice. These themes are presented in the table below and described in the following sections, where we embed comments from contributors to provide a sense of the depth, scope, and scale of each of the themes. Contributors' comments identified issues and challenges relating to ethics in the psychological professions. Each contributor brought a unique perspective, communicating contemporary and historical matters that generate current challenges.

Each of the themes identified below can be viewed on a spectrum, from problematic phenomena and situations, through to areas of ethical practice largely missing from published literature, to representation of positive aspects of relational ethics and the presence of hope to move forward positively and productively with relational ethics for counselling and helping professions.

Box 2.2 Key themes associated with contemporary ethical contexts and challenges

1. Training to develop reflexive ethical literacy.
2. Living and relating in complex micro and macro relational, social, cultural, and professional contexts.
3. Recognising and acknowledging personal, relational, and organisational responsibilities.
4. EDI and decolonisation of ethics theories and practices.
5. Employment for counsellors and psychotherapists.
6. Digital technologies, AI, and the counselling professions.
7. Politics in the profession and beyond.

---

1 Training to develop reflexive ethical literacy

By far the largest theme, reflexive ethical literacy was conveyed as a crucial component by all contributors. The teaching and learning of practice and helping ethics must be engaging and accessible and based upon real-life complexity and nuanced experiencing and perceiving. The importance of recognising a place and a time for the appropriate use of codes of practice and ethical frameworks was important and they needed to be considered in their own place and within the context of each unique client's/therapist's dynamics and settings.

Making ethics realistic and relatable was important to contributors and the centrality of training and placements was noted. Training was seen as a key context in which trainee practitioners could learn about ethics in practice. Trainees need to be able to recognise the centrality of anti-oppressive practice, the importance of understanding social justice and epistemic trust. Essentially, being reflexively aware of people's capacity and ability to trust in the relational context of counselling and helping and how meaning-making and decision-making in any given therapeutic context is conducted – or rather, co-conducted and co-constructed – was crucial.

It was recognised that the 'mix' and intersectionality that plays out for and between clients and therapists, would be unique to each therapeutic context and in relation to any given client/therapist dyad, group or organisation. Collaboration between clients and practitioners for mutual formulation of therapy work and processes is important. There was recognition of the value of viewing multiple dimensions of relational ethics – bringing a micro/macro, in here/out there, internal/external perspective to the work and relationships. All these factors need to be accommodated in training and development activities and aimed at being able to work with an embedded ethics approach. Importantly, trainees need to learn about developing the courage and conviction to trust the client and the relational therapeutic processes, as Rich notes:

> . . . there's something here about the clients say "nah, Rich, you're on the total wrong thing". I say, well, I'm really glad you could tell me, because that means that you're able to tell me and I like hearing your view and something new is born. And I'm not sure if we always have that ability. (Rich)
> . . . initially sprung from a medical model in place, where we should be separate, we should have this one, we should have this dynamic in place, whereas now, as we sit here, there are hundreds of models out there, massive amounts of different ways in which we practice, but yet I wonder how many times we've gone back to that core tenet that actually says hang on a minute, should we be turning it around, and saying, do you know I absolutely love your Doc Martens. (Rich)

Rich conveys the challenge of authentic and ethical relating as we navigate being congruent with clients, and, by implication, the importance of learning about them during our core practitioner training:

> I think it is a revolving door relationship in which we look into the honour of a client's life and they also in my experience, should

also have the reciprocity of the equal, the equity to be able to look into ours, however in self-disclosure, which I'll probably come onto later, which is another thing that again traditionally we said we are a blank screen, we do not share about our life. We do not bring those elements into the room. (Rich)

Peter highlights the importance of developing our internal locus of evaluation, to foster our ability to sustain ourself and our decision-making in practice:

> Supporting practitioners to have a more internal locus of evaluation when thinking about their own practice, or how can we support a therapist to reflect and assess their competence, their prejudices themselves, and not necessarily rely on external people like supervisors, or your professional body, or additional training courses. (Peter)

Of course, no training programme can ever include absolutely everything a practitioner could possibly know about the underlying theoretical premises of the training approach or the multidimensional ways in which those premises could be articulated in day-to-day practice. That said, there are certainly areas that should be encompassed in a core curriculum, as colleagues have signposted below, beginning with a comment from Alistair:

> [I] know this came up in our conversation at the BACP research conference, you know, we do have to train the trainers . . . it's the people who are doing the, you know, training in relationship to this and yet we also have to be utterly pragmatic which is that on any training course that you're only going to get you know, one or two or three options to talk about ethics? (Alistair)
> I think there's a real challenge for the individual practitioner to find their way and know what they're doing in a way that's consistent with their professional frameworks but also that's responsive to the particular client they have . . . I mean I think if I had to say one word which I think is the key, I think we need to be reflexive. (Linda)
> A lot of the things that need to be covered could be just uploaded and students can read. It's not necessarily stuff that we have to be doing in the classroom with them in groups, but to do more of this experiential stuff in groups with people would take much more time and awareness and emotional energy from the

tutors. And I don't know, I think most environments are such that there are too few people doing too much work with too many. (Gillian)

. . . very few courses that I've come across actually look at what is it to be human. (Alistair)

How do we describe this in a way that helps the therapist think sensibly about themselves and the work that they do and think that ...by attending to this they actually can make a huge difference incrementally within the society in which they operate. (Hadyn)

The reason we've got to this place is because we, there is very little philosophical understanding about the nature of who and what we do and why.(Alistair)

. . . the kinds of issues clients are coming with are created in a relational context . . . and any healing has to take place in a relational context. (Linda)

. . . increase people's awareness of their own places of fear, really, to hopefully get to know, recognise, go to those places to be able to come away and then try and go somewhere else...educate people as to what happens when you go to that place and how to mindfully be able to come out of it. (Gillian)

. . . the ground shifts underneath them, all of a sudden, the idea of this 'what do you do, and how do you do it, what do you get, and what happens when you do A, B and C?' (Dwight)

. . . training courses have to be more up to being able to deliver a training that serves different counsellors and different client groups. (Gillian)

Perhaps an important point to highlight in relation to training is that courses could convey, from the outset, the inevitability that as trainees we may feel defensive or threatened, or even triggered, when we encounter the complexities of working in the counselling and helping professions. As Gillian comments:

And I do that more and more in my teaching, kind of predicting that the first response I'm gonna get is going to be defensive and the "what I need to do" is almost getting there before that, try and get some information out to students to be able to read something about the defensive places that people go to commonly and how that's really normal. And of course, people don't wanna be seen this way. (Gillian)

Contributor colleagues all convey the centrality of training content on 'self as practitioner' and the importance of working reflexively, non-defensively, and being mindful that inclusive, non-oppressive and compassionate care is central to the work. And yet, in the context of a curriculum that is full of theoretical content, how feasible is that? Clearly, the personal and professional development of the trainee is paramount; with the proviso that trainees are equally learning about the core relational skills required, concurrent with finding out more about their own relational defences and triggers.

Importantly, we need to recognise the personal journey involved in developing the capacity, reflexivity, and responsiveness for practice, as Rich conveys:

> I think it's really important that that hasn't come about easily. It's come from a journey of getting it wrong and learning and realising from getting it wrong and that it's okay to get things wrong. But I'm not sure how often in the profession we say that. (Rich)
>
> Sometimes our clients ask for direction, sometimes our clients want the support in taking steps, and I think sometimes we use self-disclosure. We think that it only relies on what we share of our lives, whereas as a disabled practitioner I wheel into a room and I'm automatically disclosing that I'm disabled. There are many things that we disclose about ourselves. (Rich)

Peter emphasised the importance of taking time to embed our core training, the concepts we learn about, and our ways of being in our practice, and doing this prior to training in other approaches or modalities.

> . . . there's a real risk that people are gathering all these tools, but they're not embedding how they, how are they going to use them, how is that going to work in practice? (Peter)

2 Living and relating in complex micro and macro relational, social, cultural, and professional contexts

Therapy does not exist in a vacuum. It is not simply the hour of counselling, or the group intervention, or whatever other therapeutic offer is being made. People exist within political, social, cultural, familial, professional, and organisational systems and stigmas. We also live in a global society traumatised by legacy of the recent Covid-19 pandemic. Moreover, we live in a competitive and neo-liberal 21st century, in which phenomena and factors intersect, often with oppressive and limiting consequences for citizens.

Our clients, as do we, inevitably bring social, cultural, and relational influences as well as impacts from trauma, from corrupt or toxic systems, and from the consequences of injustices, into the therapeutic room, work, relational dynamics, and practice contexts. As Linda states:

> We can no longer get away with practising as individuals behind closed doors . . . there is a wider socio-political context that we need [to acknowledge] and cultural contexts that we need to consider. So, I think that's not really one challenge, but it's a context of multiple challenges. So that's one thing. I think in a micro level, in terms of the relationship between client and therapist . . . it's the biggest issue. Seems to me that what comes up again and again and again, particularly with supervisees, is around boundaries and the confusion of that . . . self-disclosure or touch or you know 'what do I do in this situation?' (Linda)
>
> [Ethics] . . . is the means by which I govern myself in relation to those I'm with . . . whichever community and context I'm in . . . that I govern my behaviour, I govern my impulses, I govern my ID. It is the way I might use my superego creatively rather than destructively. It is that level of self-awareness, it is the supervisor. I listen to that. I work hard to have on my shoulder. It is those things where I work really hard to listen carefully to what I'm about to say to someone and actually "does it fit within the context in a healthy way?" That's what ethics is for me. (Hadyn)
>
> We have internal challenges such as the union across our profession, and of the many different levels of highly qualified professionals that come together in very different ways and means to meet clients and provide services and therapy. We also then have external threats and challenges that come with the invention of artificial intelligence. (Rich)
>
> . . . there's too much of, well, you know, this is what I do, but this is not what I am. (Hadyn)

As Hadyn pointedly highlights, surely, what we do is who we are? Dwight rightly challenges the professions with the reality that

> . . . that whole idea of actually things don't stay static . . . how do they see their position with regards to keeping the relational flow of ethics within the therapeutic space? . . . it's that relational understanding of the relational dynamics that then creates a constantly evolving ethical framework for ourselves, for our clients, for our profession, and having that regular dialogue, seeing it as a fluid construct and not just something defined by the organisations [professional bodies]. (Dwight)

John highlighted the importance of research and evidence-building work in counselling, as well as the hidden investigation and relational research that plays out in the collaborative co-production of the therapy relationship.

> Counsellors and psychotherapists are actually researchers, whether it's formalised or [informal] research. But just the very nature of the way that we work and the way we're with our client, and we're collaborating, and we're continually hypothesising, and sharing our thoughts with our clients and so on, that good practice is essentially that we're constantly researching and I'm always talking with clients about [that], and when I'm teaching as well, about the concept of mutual curiosity, that I find that really important. So, so I think essentially that good practice actually is, it's research. (John)

3 Recognising and acknowledging personal, relational, and organisational responsibilities

There are tensions between adhering to prescriptive ethics codes and 'rules' and the taking of personal and relational responsibility to navigate, relationally, through the complexities and nuances of being a human in helping relationships, work, and processes. How do we understand and work with therapy concepts that are not universally acknowledged or believed? For example, not all practitioners would subscribe to psychoanalytical or psychodynamic concepts such as narcissism, or transference and countertransference. How can we navigate complex conceptual terrain? Endeavouring to respond to such questions forms part of the 'backbone' of relational ethics.

What do we as practitioners regard as 'practice ethics' and how do we forge ethical virtues and commitments? The contributor comments below illuminate a range of questions, challenges, concepts, and tensions evident in this complex helping landscape, including whether and how research can or does inform ethics in practice.

Don't check your humanity at the door of the session. Take your humanity and who you are into the room. Use those as therapeutic tools. Don't underestimate the power of lived experience and the ability for it to be something else that a person can relate with . . . When we go into that room trying to be something we're not, we encourage our clients to do the same and that is the life of trauma that I believe they've always lived. (Rich)

What, actually, is within our remit . . . as ethics or ethical practice, and what sits on the other side of that boundary? And I think the greatest challenge in the profession when it comes to ethics is where do we draw that line, what's included and what's excluded? . . . I think I know where my boundary is . . . what I often get back . . . when I put posts out there on social media to say their therapy is political therapy . . . that's a boundary that often gets challenged by other practitioners who say "no politics doesn't belong in the space" or "what's going on out there doesn't belong in this space, it's about the individual". And I go well the individual, you can't take the individual out of that external context. (Myira)

. . . to build the relationships and allow the understandings to happen then that sort of ethical component of how people relate to each other, understand one another, is the thing that becomes the source of healing and movement and development as a human being. (Hadyn)

. . . being a responsible person means taking responsible responsibility for how we are in the world relationally with people, with the world, with the environment, with organisations, with everything . . . giving that responsibility to something else is fundamentally suspect. (Gillian)

The consequences of a breakdown of relationships centuries ago, which remain imbued within the culture and the cultures of that of that fragile society, and there's still reaping the whirlwind of that, and the failure in time. And again, whether it's at an institutional level, organisational level, or global level, is the failure

to realise that you have to pay attention to those relationships between people and the ethics. (Hadyn)
    . . . recognise that [professional bodies] are potentially part of
the problem. How would you take [members] money and use those
resources to shift it? . . . how do you shift this vast ocean-going
liner out on the high seas? How do you get it gradually to turn
around and come back to a sort of safer harbour, more ethical
way of being . . . turn around the profession, where the focus becomes the profession and those who are served by the profession.
(Hadyn)
    So I think one of the biggest things for me is that counsellors
themselves don't always recognise how important research is.
And I don't, I think the profession for too long has ignored the
possibilities of research. (John)
    Part of that collaboration [with participants or clients] is shar-
ing with them, sharing what I've written, sharing and sharing
data with them. Checking it's OK, checking that my observations
match what they think I should be watching, see, yeah. I think the
contact process I think is constantly doing . . . (John)
    I mean, I wonder if it's about, you and I have talked about this
before, it's not about tick boxes and protocols, it's about a mindset
of always being aware of where you are in the position of power
with the person that you're working with and doing your very best
to ameliorate that power imbalance. (John)
    And I think it's only over time as you get more experienced, do
we do we then it's individual practitioners are we able to loosen
those boundaries ourselves. But I do recognise though that I
think there is a proportion of the profession, of practitioners that
kind of feel more contained and held by what feels like fairly explicit binary rigid ethical boundaries because then there's a very
clear sense of what's right and what's wrong, what's ethical, what's
unethical . . . I think it's about a level of confidence in the practitioner to feel like at what point can I start to loosen? (Myira)
    I guess you can harm different people in different ways, a lot
of it again is around that kind of pluralistic approach where you
work closely with the clients or the research subject to offer some
you know some degree of choice . . . and I'm aware sometimes
it's difficult to get that balance right. You know, I strive to all the
time, and again, it's around constantly . . . checking with them.
(John)

Practitioner fear, defensiveness, and narcissism were recognised by some. It was acknowledged that defensive fear can block engagement with relational ethics. It can also prevent constructive and collaborative conversation. Some thought that narcissistic practitioners, professions, and professional bodies were problematic at times. Whilst recognising that all humans could probably be located somewhere along a narcissism spectrum, there was concern about striving for and providing genuine care and compassion for oppressed, excluded, misrepresented, and disadvantaged peoples. Associated self-awareness and endeavouring to understand self and self in relation to others, featured in research conversations.

That it is only with that depth of self-awareness and continued commitment to your own self-awareness, whether that's forming your own groups with like-minded practitioners to help you remain fully aware so that your way of being isn't just something that you artificially assume as a mantle when you walk into the room . . . it's something that you live and breathe, but it's who you are that you challenge at every turn. (Hadyn)
    . . . the reason we've got to this place is because we, there is very little philosophical understanding about the nature of who and what we are and why . . . I think the biggest ethical challenge is the narcissism of therapists. (Alistair)
    . . . there's so many examples I've seen where it hasn't been a faintest trace of hope that someone has even attempted to understand themselves in any depth and yet feel they can work with highly complex issues which often are born out of dysfunctional relational dynamics in their client's past and history. (Hadyn)
    So, what happens is that they construct their own little world in their own consulting room. It and a user, whatever therapeutic space that use, are not privileging a particular room and everything becomes very self-centred. So, ethics is something they that they're not really that interested in until impinges on their world and the idea of there might be values, principles, practices that are beyond them, they're not really interested in, you know, it's, and I know you'll have done this, but if you've ever tried to manage a group of counsellors. (Alistair)
    So, if Freud was starting to work today, he wouldn't have used Oedipus . . . he'd use the story of Narcissus as the Greek myth that

has the greatest relevance to how you know how we are, you know, and what, what is it like when there is no mirror? (Alistair)

. . . I am with Hienz Kohut, who would say that there is a necessary narcissism . . . it's not all pathological but what gets rewarded is the kind of, uh, but that's the nature of media. (Alistair)

Importantly, we cannot overestimate the process of adjustment as we realise the magnitude of developing our own inner relational ethic. As Dwight notes:

> . . . the shift that students often have to go through between being prescriptive of what the rules are . . . versus taking personal responsibility and that personal thought process that goes with actually developing their own internalised ethical framework and the journey they go through. (Dwight)

Hierarchical tensions do exist in the social, relational, and cultural aspects of the helping professions, with disparities of perceptions about what constitutes a working professional; however, we would do well as practitioners to enable our clients or patients to understand that all humans are flawed, as Rich notes:

> . . . know that they are not the only broken one amongst a fixed community, that we as human beings are broken. (Rich)

Significantly, we need to be able to make clinical and professional decisions about the wellbeing and safeguarding of individuals we work with, paying mindful attention to the importance of enabling individuals to talk with us about their distress and despair:

> People come into our rooms that are hopeless, that are suicidal, that wish pain to stop, that want a space in which they can look at these elements . . . Not immediately be safeguarded. They wish a safe space in which they can be held. (Rich)

4 Inclusivity and decolonisation of ethics theories and practices

A central tenet across research conversations is that EDI (Equality, Diversity, Inclusivity) is essential, alongside adopting core principles of compassion, collaboration, co-production, consultation, inclusivity, social justice, and the prevention of 'othering' of any kind in our navigation of relational ethics. The whole notion of decolonisation of ethics concepts and practices was recognised by contributors as an area needing authentic and ongoing work in the counselling and mental health professions. It was also an area that until recently was missing from the philosophical and ethics literature and as with other areas identified from the research conversation, warrant work, research, and publications. Given that there are challenges in embedding ethics concepts and resources into day-to-day practice, as some see ethics codes and guidelines as shelf items that are only referred to when risk or safeguarding issues arise,

So, things being called out a lot more, I think, and colonialism being on the agenda. You know, all those things are talked about a lot more and I think it's really a, you know, we're barely off the starting line, you know to actually think what that means for us individually, in our relationships, for the profession, for institutions, is with you know, with so much work to do. But the fact that it is started and being recognised as a problem has got to be a good thing, surely. (Gillian)

Deconstructing ethical models derived from dominant practice ethics literature is essential. Predominantly medicalised, Eurocentric, white, westernised, paternalistic, and oppressive, the underpinning philosophical and epistemological framework needs deconstructing, with a view to identifying an ethical framework that acknowledges non-westernised approaches to ethics. Developing anti-oppressive concepts, practices, and processes for relationships in the counselling and mental health professions is necessary. How can we develop a decolonised relational ethic without recourse to the dominant approach to professional ethics? We need to mine sources that offer compassionate and relational ways of being, as Dwight indicates.

I was actually writing this morning on that topic of decolonisation, cause it's not as simple as just putting some new books on a shelf. And whatever else, it's we you both understand this, so it's a massive topic area. You're talking about hundreds if not thousands of years of learning ethics . . . OK, let me just, thinking off my head as I write some notes to myself. We'll talk about the relational and ethics. You mentioned pluralism as well. The 'what relationship means from a non-westernised perspective' is slightly different thing. Our interconnectedness with things. Then the more, the thing about colonisation is, it's quite objectifying of the other . . . Where it's built between two people or a group or whatever it is, that brings us more into a more relational framework. Just sort of sits outside of the sort of Western philosophical paradigm. (Dwight)

Sources of pragmatic inspiration that can provide non-westernised or non-Eurocentric perspectives can be found. For example, matriarchal cultures have been characterised by their relational, gender, and socially egalitarian ways of being, living, working, and relating. Their societies tend to demonstrate a 'power with' culture, rather than a Eurocentric and westernised patriarchal and objectifying 'power over' culture. Philosophical sources can also be found, including through indigenous cultures and faiths such as Tibetan Buddhism.

EDI in UK counselling professions is, currently, largely evident at the level of strategy and principles. What is missing and much needed are processes of embedding inclusivity and anti-oppressive practices into all aspects of work, life, living, relating, and organisational contexts.

. . . statements of welcoming diversity do nothing. You know, it just obscures the problem, rather than saying we recognise we have a problem in this profession . . . racism is endemic in everything. (Gillian)

Understanding the nature and impact of intersecting injustices or oppression is crucial knowledge that all practitioners in the counselling and mental health professions need to be aware of. Additionally, we need to consider intersecting influences brought into dyadic, group, or systems work by both clients and practitioners.

. . . what you do with one client may be different from another. My being with one client may be different from my being with another client . . . think if you're working relationally, and relational ethics, you're thinking about the client, the therapist, and what's going on between, and you're thinking of the social context in which the three are embedded . . . you're attending to it all . . .

I like intersectionality as a concept in that, you know, we're complicated you know, different levels of power and powerlessness . . .
(Linda)

5 Employment for counsellors and psychotherapists

There are evidently insufficient employment opportunities for counsellors and psychotherapists, as well as potential exploitation through ongoing proliferation of voluntary placements for trainees and trained practitioners. Tensions between seeking a vocation and a job were identified as a feature of the current employment opportunities – or rather lack of – in the professions. Further conflicts between the need to generate an income to survive and hopefully thrive and that of wanting to translate training and development into an offer of a quality professional service were evident.

Another dimension associated with employment opportunities for counselling and psychotherapists is recognition of the annual numbers of people being trained. That and the tensions and realities of a counselling profession's landscape where we have counsellors, psychotherapists, counselling psychologists and clinical psychologists competing for employment opportunities in organisational and mental health contexts. Many more people are entering training, as Gillian states:

> . . . more and more younger people are going into this work as a profession . . . and that's right, you know, it's a profession and it also requires far more than we will ever be paid for . . . I think the only regulation we can ever trust is our own sense of our own integrity. And the only way to have any say about that is to make sure that that's really prioritised throughout all the training and throughout the structures that work for counsellors to practice.
> (Gillian)

6 Digital technologies and AI

6.i Online video counselling: Learning about the context and identifying what works for whom, with what type of presentation/issue was evident, as were the needs to be aware of the space, and the impact of the online context for both the practitioner(s) and the client(s).

Consideration of appearance and backdrop, including the practitioner's own appearance were thought to be important. Consideration of eye contact and conversations between practitioner and client need to be explored and agreed. Collaboratively negotiated and agreed boundaries were important, as was awareness of professional body guidance and training courses available to prepare practitioners for online work.

> I think the world is changing and we see online work . . . I think there are a whole load of new ethical issues that we haven't perhaps thought about enough. That. That that's all part of the new, the New World. And I think it just generally increases the diversity around [practice] and I think if you understand ethics as I do, as totally depending on the relational and the broader social context, this makes a difference. (Linda)

6.ii Social media platforms: Complex challenges and a potentially toxic environment make it important to have clear behavioural and relational boundaries on social media. Social media platforms can and are used positively. In some ways, paradoxically, social media gives more opportunity for discourse and dialogue. Practitioner awareness of their social media presence and contributions was important, including the impact on past, current, or future clients. Clients nowadays are more likely to search for their practitioner online and on social media platforms, hence the need for practitioner awareness and reasoned decisions about how they choose to be visible and engaged in these public domains. Additionally, younger generations are familiar with social media platform where many relationships play out and communities of likeminded individuals are formed. Interactions tend to occur now, in the moment and there is no depth or sustained dialogues exploring intentionality, content or meaning making.

Peter talked about the challenges we face where we have public facing social media accounts, and some of the issues posed for our client work.

> To not cross those boundaries I suppose, because clients will be looking and watching things I'm doing. So, I'm talking about therapy and they're having therapy with me. It's kind of those issues are going to come up whether they like what I've said or whether they don't like what I've said . . . so that can be a real difficult

balance and I think one of the things that I find difficult is a lot of the guidance from the membership bodies is about not making personal disclosures online. I don't know how you do that. (Peter)
I talk about counselling and psychotherapy and other professions online. And you know, 'if you come across anything and you want to talk about it' then it's an invitation to kind of do that . . . Generally, clients don't tend to bring it and discuss it, but they appreciate the conversation. (Peter).

Alistair and Dwight convey the challenges of appropriate behaviour and posts on social media, whilst Linda notes how young people are familiar with social media platforms and tend to use them frequently.

So, the culture of media has changed, but also social media . . . but the shadow side of it is, is that it's very self-referential, you know, nobody's accountable to anything. The real issue is 'am I liked, or am I not liked?' . . . Move away from a values-based system into a much more pragmatic, what's in it for me, and the value-based system implies, that has an implicit notion, of community and society. So, I think we've lost that sense that we're part of it. We're part of a community. What we've replaced that with is a meet, a social media community, so we've recreated community but it's, but it's a community in our own image. So, the whole notion of social media is, it's all about me. (Alistair)
. . . young people are so used to being on social media . . . (Linda)
The negative side of it, of therapists or of practitioners talking about their client, work on social media, because that's just a no go umm. But even that then brings up issues about OK, what is OK to talk about and what is not OK to talk about? How much does one get involved in that whole area? Because it can be quite toxic. There's that side of things. (Dwight)

6.iii Responding to rapid technological development: We cannot ignore technological advances; we just need to critically consider how we advance in ways that are meaningful and hold value for the counselling and mental health professions and their clients. Further evidence and research are needed on the challenges and opportunities provided by digitisation and AI. Whilst social media provides an important medium through which to connect and share, it can also be toxic. Trolls instigating hostility and aggression have created harmful, sometimes deadly, consequences. Given the potential for harm, there is no doubt that social media and AI present the next big challenge for relational ethics.

> It's a key issue for us, that how do we deal with how we imbue artificial intelligence with relational ethics . . . If we see that the whole, the whole, centrality, what it is to be human, and to be healthy, and to grow and develop, actually is through those relationships and the development of the relationship of one person to another, and getting it right, is that the means by which someone can improve and develop. How on earth can we get that into artificial intelligence when artificial intelligence is being heralded as the way in which economically [viable] therapy can be delivered on mass to people who need it? . . . Yes, perhaps artificial intelligence can answer those questions, but I'm not sure it can take a client any further than that and I become really anxious about what gets perpetuated through that artificial intelligence and who is it, who is feeding the artificial intelligence that become the resource?
> (Hadyn)

The professions need the 'how to' of working and relating through online media and with regards to how AI is integrated into counselling and helping work. Practice needs a safe frame, privacy, and safety in relation to the online work and prompts many questions including, for example, in relation to online work, is the session secure? Who is around? Can the client have privacy in their home or other online space? Can they be heard by others? What impact does a move from the online session back into usual space/place/people have upon clients and practitioners? How can we use technology competently. What eye contact can be achieved or desired when working online? Are there particular needs or presentations that clients might have? For example, there are challenges working with young people online as they are so used to being on social media and using WhatsApp that the therapy can become simply as if it's just like another zoom call with a friend. Additional factors include specific contracting for online working including contingencies if technology fails, such as a 'plan B' to connect via telephone, or whether the session can be extended if technology issues arise and interrupt the session times. Whilst professional bodies offer competencies or guidance in relation to online working, training must also provide a context in which online, digital and AI work can be explored and experienced through case studies and live examples, as well as through evidence and research informed decisions about whether and how to use digitised or AI technologies.

7 Politics in the profession and beyond

Micro- and macro-level political contexts were evident, with evidence of challenges faced in NHS contexts and those involving professional bodies. One contributor who had worked within NHS contexts, described them as environments not conducive to relational ethics. Their concern about the medical model and that the pathologising of people within a medicalised conceptualisation of mental health undermined humanistic approaches to interventions was palpable. They also considered the oppressive powerplays that operated within NHS and other organisational contexts, highlighting inequities in UK culture, politics, and societies.

Below, Gillian concisely and compellingly narrates some of the challenges that individuals and the professions need to engage with when working in organisational and politicised environments like the NHS:

> . . . how to work in a society that's so full of inequalities . . . the people who are training to be counsellors are going to be the most privileged. So, the difference between the people who are offering and the people who are receiving it just gets bigger and bigger.
> . . . it became increasingly clear to me how impossible it is . . . how extremely challenging and at what a big cost. It came to counsellors trying to hold on to relational ethics . . . I don't know how people do it now . . . so I think there's very few safe spaces left that where the organisations enable counsellors to hold on to relational values and valuing the clients they're working with . . . so I think working ethically or relationally in that context, I don't know how people do it now . . . I think there's few safe spaces left where the organisations enable counsellor to hold onto relational values and valuing the clients they're working with.
> . . . You know, all these medical ideas that counselling has kind of bought into to some extent to get a place at the table in medical services but has ended up biting in the foot because it just makes no sense. It's where all the requirements for RCTs in research come from, assuming we're medical and it's, it just makes

nonsense of the relational endeavour that we're trying to do . . .
another thing to do with organisations that make it very difficult
for counsellors to work ethically is the medicalisation of counselling and so it's not just the economic commodification of it all and
the clients becoming numbers, it's assuming that mental distress
is like a pathology, a disease that is just treated, that counsellors
are interchangeable . . .

. . . I guess it's like the counselling profession is in the world
where mental health isn't taken seriously, and this profession
isn't taken seriously. What it takes to train people to take this
all seriously, isn't taken seriously, and given enough resources
to do it.

. . . what we all do individually depends on who we are, how
we are situated, what feels possible, what inspires us, what influence we have in different circles. What suits us? It's now. It's like
we're not short of things to try and change our way, you know?
And we've gotta look after ourselves as well as in that process to
be able to then respond relationally to the people who come into
our most immediate sphere of influence, in a way that's different.
(Gillian)

Of course, oppression and misdirected use of professional and re-
searcher power do not just occur within dyadic or group interventions,
they traverse all sections of the counselling and helping professions,
including research, as John highlights:

People like John McLeod are doing so well, Robert Elliott and
so on ... trying to move us away from this hierarchy of research
importance and, you know, research value in a sort of "we'll start
with the randomised controlled trial and then we gotta move down
and somewhere at the bottom is the case study". And I think, I
think we still need to really work hard at a political level to change
that and to give some equal value. (John)

Of significance in the UK, in relation to micro and macro politics, is
the employment of counsellors and psychotherapists. In the UK, the
counselling professions include counselling, psychotherapy, counselling psychology and clinical psychology. Counselling psychology and
clinical psychology are subjected to statutory regulation through the
Health and Care Professions Council (HCPC), whilst counsellors and

psychotherapists participate in a voluntary registration scheme, approved by the Professional Standards Authority (PSA), whereby professional bodies can apply to host a PSA accredited registrar within their organisation. Professional bodies pay a fee to PSA to host the register and trained practitioners can apply to be entered on the register to denote their upholding of professional standards and public safety. PSA is the supra-regulator in the UK, overseeing multiple regulatory bodies including the General Medical Council (GMC) and the HCPC. There are differing opinions on the status of each of the professional areas that fall under the title counselling professions. It is widely recognised that those subject to statutory regulation (practitioner psychologists) are perceived as being of a higher professional status than counsellors and psychotherapists who fall within the lighter touch voluntary registration.

Typically, many counsellors work in private practice or in voluntary roles, as paid employment within an organisational context is limited. Whilst philanthropic practice is an honourable choice for some, for others, cost-of-living challenges mean a living wage is essential. Earning a living and providing quality care are not mutually exclusive. The counselling employment situation in the UK has generated inequities and misperceptions, and fostered degrees of hostility in the counselling professions. The UK professional body British Association for Counselling and Psychotherapy, worked in collaboration with other key UK professional bodies to develop the SCoPED (scope of practice and education) framework, which aims to offer a way of identifying counsellor and psychotherapist roles and associated competencies, similar to HCPC professional practitioner protocols. However, SCoPED is contested; not least in relation to what is regarded as a negative distinction between counselling and psychotherapy, setting in place a hierarchy of roles. Hopefully, the professional body consortium that developed the framework will provide opportunities for non-defensive and open dialogue on SCoPED as it begins to influence UK training and practice. Whether it influences counsellor and psychotherapist employment opportunities remains to be seen.

Sociopolitical influences within the UK labour market have seen an increase in counsellor and psychotherapist job opportunities, however employment is limited and there are significant concerns around the volunteer culture that grew around counsellor training and post-training practice. As Peter identifies, there are tensions evident in counselling contexts where trainee practitioners accrue required training practice hours. Peter notes:

> 'And we don't want you to leave once you've got, you know, your 100 hours or whatever' and you can understand it in part, from an organisational point of view. But at the same time, these people have given their time for free, for free. (Peter)
> Sometimes it feels within the bigger organisations that change can be really slow and I feel like some of the innovative practice is actually happening outside of those organisations, in groups and communities of therapists that are kind of setting up and they're pushing and driving for change and some of the organisations are a bit slow in terms of how they respond to that and they understand these issues to do with funding and structures . . . (Peter)
> Working in those big organisations, it's quite difficult not to become corporatised . . . But if you truly foster an environment of debate and discussion and openness, you can still you can still have people who have to deliver what the organisation decides but it creates a different type of environment for therapists to talk about how they think the profession should be. (Peter)

Peter also highlighted how different therapeutic modalities can encounter or foster unhelpful stereotypes and misunderstandings of therapeutic approaches. For example, person-centred counselling can be seen as apathetic and shallow, whereas in reality, the approach provides compassion, challenge, and change opportunities in the context of an inclusive and respectful therapy relationship.

Chapter conclusion

Evident from rich contributions made by the research contributors, the reality is that the relational ethics landscape is a complex and contested one. Our contributors have eloquently and richly portrayed just how challenging it is to navigate this landscape. The themes developed from our research conversations with contributors were: training to develop reflexive ethical literacy; living and relating in complex micro and macro relational, social, cultural, and professional contexts; recognising and acknowledging personal, relational, and organisational responsibilities; EDI and decolonisation of ethics theories and practices; digital technologies, AI, and the counselling professions; and politics in the profession and beyond (including practitioner employment). These themes capture the multidimensional areas that practitioners, professional bodies, and training organisations need to be able to reflexively comprehend in the context of day-to-day practice settings. Research and perspectives papers related to each of the thematic areas is needed and, given their socio-psycho-politico dimensions, interdisciplinary inquiry is vital.

Radical recognition of the importance of embedding ethics in our behaviours, ways of relating, meaning making, and decision making is fundamental to contemporary ethics for counselling and helping practice. What is also crystal clear from our research conversations is the reality that ethics in practice is not, cannot be, and never should be, mechanistic or narrowly manualised areas of practice. More realistic is to aim for evidence informed ways of being that acknowledge complexity, that authentically respond to diverse social and cultural influences, that seriously challenge injustices and oppression, and that compassionately engage in the complex and relational minutiae of therapeutic thinking, reasoning, relating and practice. Importantly, the textbooks already commissioned for this Routledge series resonate with and reflect the areas identified by our research contributors, offering valuable affirmation for this innovative body of work.

Reference

Braun, V. & Clarke, C. (2021). *Thematic Analysis: A Practical Guide.* Sage.

Chapter 3

Thinking about ethics in practice

This chapter sets out key theories, concepts, and contemporary challenges in practice ethics. It offers multiple lenses through which to make meaning of complex practice or risk scenarios and settings. The chapter engages with the complexities of ethical codes, frameworks, and theories, whilst capturing the challenges and reality of day-to-day meaning-making, decision-making, and associated practices. In essence, the chapter outlines practice examples, demonstrating how to translate information from ethical codes, frameworks, and resources, into day-to-day work as practitioners.

Introduction

In Chapters 1 and 2 we set the scene for what we mean by ethics, while additionally drawing on some contemporary key thinkers in the field of counselling and psychotherapy to help further develop our own thinking and bring in a broader context to our writing. As we are already encountering, ethics sits within a pluralistic frame in that it can mean different things to different people, at different times. It is particularly challenging, therefore, to think about how we transition from the theory of ethics into the application of ethics in our work with clients.

While the concept of *theory to practice* is not in and of itself new to most readers of this book (given it is an oft-used phrased to consider how we translate the theory of the modality of our training into the therapeutic process with clients), the challenge of making this jump from the conceptual to the practical with ethics can feel much more daunting. In this context, therefore, there are perhaps several misconceptions that need attending to, before then moving on to how we can embrace the concepts of relational ethics into our day-to-day work in subsequent chapters, to support ourselves and our clients alike.

DOI: 10.4324/9781003354970-3

This chapter will begin by considering some key misconceptions we, as authors, have heard over the years before then taking a more positive (and hopefully encouraging) position with a '*how do we*' approach to relational ethics, as opposed to a '*why should we*' position, which can often speak of anxiety or uncertainty in navigating this important process. The latter stages of the chapter will then look specifically at ways in which we can use the concepts of relational ethics to not only support our own thinking in practice, but more excitingly to reflect on how we may collaboratively agree an ethical position with our clients.

Here, our assertion will be that while some ethical decisions might need to be made before the client walks into the room (or logs on online), beyond these broader parameters we can work actively and collaboratively to create an ethical narrative that supports the relationship we have with our clients, and respects the diversity and difference in perspective and personhood we might encounter to ensure all voices are captured in that narrative. Before we begin on that exciting and innovative exploration, however, let's deal with some of the misconceptions that might otherwise get in the way.

Ethics and misconceptions

Both of us have worked at the heart of professional associations over many years and, by virtue of those roles, have had the opportunity to see the chasm that can often exist between those who are immersed in the production of ethics – from codes through to frameworks – and those who sign up to work within those ethical parameters when they join, but then perhaps never explicitly think of ethics again. We say 'explicitly', because our assertion here is not that those who don't regularly read their ethical guidelines are unethical, because that could not be further from the truth in our thinking. But there is a difference in working intuitively in the best interests of the client and the therapeutic relationship, and engaging with the vast array of ethical possibilities in the therapeutic encounter at a more explicit level. In one way, this is our hope in writing this book – and editing this book series; that we can encourage practitioners to be more excited about the possibilities that ethical engagement can provide. We use the word 'excited' deliberately; this is a good place to start when thinking of some misconceptions. The key ones we will try to address are:

- Ethics is boring: there is nothing in ethics that *really* speaks to therapy itself.

- Ethics is an intellectual endeavour, best left to those with their heads in books, not in the therapy room.
- Ethics isn't really relevant to me because, fundamentally, I know the difference between right and wrong in therapy.
- Ethics is simply the mechanism that professional associations threaten you with.
- Ethics doesn't really speak to power and diversity; it is about power over the other and doing everything the same.

Think about what experiences or other factors shape your approach to thinking about ethics, and what particular positive or negative aspects are present in your own beliefs about ethics.

Ethics is boring: there is nothing in ethics that really speaks to therapy itself

There used to be a saying that people often began their counselling training as a means of accessing their own counselling – it was more a therapeutic encounter than a training and learning one. Then, once the 'feeling' stuff about building group dynamics and intrapersonal insight was over and the next module on ethics came along, it was the time to leave. In short, those who were going to leave training courses generally did so once the perceived 'boring' bit started, i.e., ethics. As Jenkins (2017, p. 132) notes, 'It is easy to see ethics as a rather dry subject. It may seem to have an earnest and rather worthy feel to it. It can also seem somehow divorced from real life and from the actual practice of counselling.' Whether this assertion is more 'urban legend' rather than actual experience is hard to say, but it is a saying built on a believable premise because, after all, everyone knows ethics is boring. Or do they?

Yet, and as we might repeat throughout this text, ethics might not be explicitly considered by many until a situation arises when we want guidance about how best to navigate it. That is, ethics might be considered boring until: we face a client experiencing suicidal thoughts; or we are working with a young person and suspect a safeguarding issue; or the boundaries of the relationship between us and our client become confused or muddied because of a change in circumstance; or we might need to consider varying our fees; or might need to suspend or end counselling because of ill-health; or . . . we could go on. There are almost unlimited possibilities where we may turn to ethics to help us negotiate or navigate a therapeutic encounter.

We can also sometimes feel frustrated when, having turned to our ethics guidance, the straightforward answer isn't there; rather, a further multitude of possibilities we feel we need to make sense of. The challenge to this misconception fundamentally, therefore, is that ethics is *everything* about therapy itself and, by deliberately and explicitly bringing ethics more into our day-to-day – or moment-by-moment – thinking, ethical concepts, ideas and positions become more potent and relevant in our work, and we become more grounded in our work because of it.

Ethics is an intellectual endeavour, best left to those with their heads in books, not in the therapy room

Ethics can be found in many disciplines and, as such, draws on a range of theoretical and philosophical frameworks. As an aspect of philosophy, ethics can be understood through the details of everyday actions and behaviours (Danchev & Ross, 2013). We often think of ethics as clearly setting out the 'rights' and 'wrongs' of our everyday actions, and this is true to a certain extent. We understand that murder as an act is illegal in terms of the law, but also it is unethical, or immoral to take an another's life. As practitioners, we often look to ethics to help us determine what we should and shouldn't do with clients; again while there is also some truth in this, ethics that underpins or informs our practice is much more complex.

In terms of the rights and wrongs of practice, we might understand some actions as a therapist to fall outside of what is deemed acceptable within the profession. For example, most would agree that it is wrong to financially exploit a client, or to engage in a sexual relationship with them. We can be reassured by what we might understand as binary ethics – clear parameters between good and bad, right and wrong. Yet, when we think about our work with clients, most of what might be challenging, difficult, or uncertain typically sits within the grey areas of ethics. While we might understand the polarities of what is right and wrong in practice, it is everything else in between that causes uncertainty (Gabriel & Casemore, 2009).

When practitioners call the ethics helpdesks of their professional associations, they are rarely looking for advice about the clear certainties of therapy. Rather, it is because they have encountered particular relational processes that perhaps might require a decision or course of action to carefully navigate. Such practitioners are motivated to seek advice because they do not wish to cause their clients – or indeed themselves – harm. Instead, they are looking for guidance to help them think about *how* they might manage a certain situation in an ethical way.

It is for these reasons that, while ethics might be rooted in and informed by academic perspectives, the *application* of ethics in our day-to-day world personally and professionally brings challenges, questions, and opportunities. We say 'opportunities' because, if something in the therapeutic process or relationship is explored through the lens of relational ethics, it might transpire that more opportunities for growth, insight, and meaning-making become apparent than had we not brought that lens to our thinking. For that reason alone, ethics is part of therapy and not simply an adjunct to it.

Ethics is simply the mechanism that professional associations threaten you with

All professional associations in the UK that hold a voluntary register approved by the Professional Standards Authority (PSA) will have an accompanying professional conduct process. In essence, this is the mechanism for when someone brings a complaint against a member of the professional association for 'misconduct'. While some do not believe such professional conduct processes offer any meaningful protection for clients, the intention is certainly to try and offer clients – or others – scrutiny when actions of therapists have been experienced as harmful.

It is not the purpose of this text to debate the rights and wrongs of such professional conduct processes, nor to outline the details of how such processes work. This latter point is important because the regulations and mechanisms that underpin professional conduct can be complex and be informed by many considerations. We only mention them here because such processes can often be experienced by practitioners – and particularly those subject to complaints by clients or others – as punitive, with dangers including reputational damage and associated high levels of stress during conduct processes.

Likewise, many have argued that such processes are unnecessary given that so few therapists would act in such a way to cause harm to others. Sadly, by virtue of both of us having worked at the heart of professional associations for many years, we both know this is not true.

Many complaints received by professional bodies relate to actions without any intention by either party to do harm to the other; some others speak of wilful harm and malpractice, for which public protection must be a priority.

More specifically, we bring it into this chapter here because, for many, professional conduct and ethics become conflated and, once again, binary, i.e., *I must be unethical if I am found guilty of professional misconduct.* There can be two important truths that sit alongside each other in this context: falling short in our professional standards might speak of practice that has been either unethical, or insufficiently considered from an ethics perspective; and careful engagement with relational ethics in our work, therefore, helps ground our practice within sound professional standards.

It is worth highlighting one dynamic here that can be unhelpful: given that ethics not only speaks to the polarities of what might be deemed acceptable, and thus all that sits between those parameters might be subject to interpretation or further sense-making, there is lots of opportunity to disagree over aspects of practice; that in itself does not make the elements of that debate unethical. For example, there seems to have been a rise over the last few years in people claiming that something is 'unethical', whereas in fact what they are saying is that they disagree with it. That might, for example, be the management of a waiting list, or the type of publicity being used to promote a practice, or a policy or procedure that speaks to a particular aspect of our work. These situations can often provoke strong responses in practitioners who might, through their own experience, or training, or modality, or ethical position, disagree strongly. Too often we have heard the cry that the particular thing being disagreed with is 'unethical', as opposed to simply being something that we disagree with.

Herein lies the joy, and challenge, of relational ethics: there is a plurality of views and beliefs, all of which have something important to contribute: they can challenge cultural and social norms, or long-established conventions of practice, or simply our preferred ways of doing things. Much of our ethical thinking is not rooted in the certainty and the given, but rather in the uncertain, unclear, and unknown. Relational ethics brings opportunity for debate and disagreement which, if worked with and tolerated, can bring about meaningful change both for our clients and for the professional.

Ethics doesn't really speak to power and diversity; it is about power over the other and doing everything the same

We would argue the exact opposite: that ethics, and particularly relational ethics, are all about power and diversity and how we navigate our therapeutic relationships in a collaborative and as equal-as-possible way (Proctor, 2014). We say 'equal-as-possible' given that we would argue the therapeutic relationship always holds some power imbalance – that one is the *therapist* and the other the *client* assumes that something is needed by one of the other (Jenkins, 2017). We could argue that social structures and process have power built into them, benignly to retain structure and process, but also with a potential to exert malignant control, such as discrimination and oppression (Proctor, 2014).

We can see the benign and malignant potential for power in our day-to-day experiences, but we would argue here that, in the context of therapy and the therapeutic relationship, we can do more than simply sit at either of these two polarities. If we exert our power over our client with a deliberate intention to control or cause harm, we are introducing a malignant force into our work. However, if we sit with power in a benign way, if we not acknowledging its existence or the social injustice that our clients might be experiencing, we may be colluding with more harm. In this context, therefore, we would argue that ethics – and relational ethics – is the structure through which we can think about and engage explicitly with in our work.

More pertinent perhaps to the criticism of ethics we are attending to here, is the notion that ethics is about *doing to*, and *doing everything the same*. Conversely, what we are suggesting is that a practitioner's engagement with ethics is about really attending to these issues so that we do not do to our clients, and relational ethics is about doing that in collaboration with our clients. If we draw on the concepts of pluralism – that people need different things at different times (Cooper & McLeod, 2010) – ethics considered in a collaborative way (also a cornerstone of pluralistic practice) ensures that our ethical position is held between therapist and client; that we talk to our clients about what ethics in therapy means, and we talk with our clients about how we can craft the most appropriate ethical position for their needs at that point, within the parameters of good practice. Herein lies the liberation of relational ethics in our work, and a vehicle through which we can embrace ethics in a way that is fundamental to our therapeutic work, rather than an abstract concept that we only refer to when we look for a right or wrong position.

What are your responses to the misconceptions outlined above? How much do you agree or disagre with the positions we have argued here?

Can you think of other misconceptions about ethics that you hold, or have heard in others?

Ethics from the periphery to the centre

The majority of practitioners in the UK are members of a professional association, perhaps to take advantage of some of their resources for continuing professional development (CPD), to participate in a practitioner community, and maybe to join a register of therapists to help secure employment (as this is often asked for by employers) and communicate a legitimacy to potential clients. At the time of writing in the UK, counselling and psychotherapy are not statutorily regulated (unlike counselling psychology, which is), and unlike other territories where there is a licensing process in place, e.g., Malta, the US. Instead, in the UK, registers are voluntarily regulated by the PSA and professional associations are register holders. For example, a practitioner may decide to join the British Association for Counselling and Psychotherapy (BACP), which is a PSA register holder, and go onto their register at different registration points.

To join a professional association and then be approved to go onto their register, it is a usual requirement that the therapist signs on their membership (or renewal) form a commitment to work to the ethics of that particular professional association; for the purposes of this discussion, we will refer to such documents as 'top-level' ethics. Each professional association calls their ethics statements something slightly different: a code, or framework, for example, but when you consider each ethics document, they all work to attend to the same issues in a similar way. Once this is all in place, the therapist will practise in whichever context of their choosing and training, e.g., a statutory agency, a school, a voluntary sector organisation, or in private practice. The same ethical document they signed up to when joining or renewing their membership applies; herein lies strength, and also weakness.

The strength of top-level ethics documents

Top-level ethics documents apply to the entire membership of the professional association and are used to set parameters of what is considered 'good' and 'poor' practice. This means that all the membership should understand what is expected of them in terms of their work as a therapist and, indeed, should also understand where actions might fall outside of ethical requirements. Professional conduct processes, therefore, draw on these top-level documents when considering complaints against their members. One key question that must be considered in the event of a complaint was whether the member acted in accordance with the ethical requirements. This is not an objective process of course; even if something is written in a top-level ethics document it can always be open to a subjective interpretation in any given situation.

What such documents do offer, however, is some sense of consistency or 'benchmark' to employing organisations and clients about the working practices of the therapist and the commitment by them to be accountable to parameters of good practice. Trust in the professional is a critical requirement for the public to consider if therapy is to be a viable option for them, particularly considering that many people access our services at times of vulnerability and trauma. Once the public loses trust in the profession, it ceases to become a viable choice for many. The existence of top-level ethics documents, and a commitment by a practitioner base to work to them, brings some stability in perception.

The weaknesses of top-level ethics documents

It could be argued that the reverse of what we have argued could constitute some of their weaknesses too. That is, they give the semblance or perception of high standards but, as they can always be interpreted and thus be subjectively applied, the perception of 'consistent' is a bit of a misnomer. Additionally, many therapists sign up to such documents at the commencement of their membership, or at renewal of membership, then rarely or never read the ethics documents again.

As such, they have given a commitment to work within the require-ments of a document they have never read. Indeed, there have been cases in professional conduct hearings where the therapist subject to a complaint has argued they didn't even realise the ethics document existed (even though they had signed to say they would work within its requirements).

In this context, therefore, such top-level documents are important and valuable to a professional association to set parameters of good practice and hold members to account in the event of a complaint but can become less relevant to a practitioner on a day-to-day basis, other than when a particular ethical or contractual challenge is encoun-tered. For many practitioners, they are perhaps important documents conceptually, but seem less relevant to the experience of working with people in the therapeutic encounter (hence some of the misconcep-tions outlined above).

This is why we have developed this series of books: to help bridge top-level ethics back into day-to-day practice, and to draw on the cen-trality of the relationship through which to achieve that; to support our ethical thinking, moving from ethics being a peripheral entity, to one where it becomes part of therapy itself. As Finlay notes, 'Ethical guidelines, although useful, can never prepare us sufficiently for situ-ations arising in practice which make our heads spin and hearts ache' (Finlay, 2019, p. 133).

Can you think of additional strengths and weaknesses of top-level ethics documents?

How do they sit in relation to your own practice, e.g., do you make regular use of ethics frameworks and codes in your day-to-day work, or are they documents you only really refer to when you encounter challenges in practice?

Relational ethics in principle

It is all very well to talk about the importance and value of relational ethics, and how such an approach can become embedded into our therapeutic thinking, without really outlining what we specifically mean. Earlier chapters have outlined our thinking here in general terms, but it is worth unpacking this concept further. There are vary-ing definitions of relational ethics and the particular components that might constitute taking this position in practice. Tomaselli et al. (2020) undertook a scoping review of the literature that explored relational ethics in the context of healthcare delivery. While here we are thinking more broadly than healthcare, there are some aspects of their review that are helpful here. They noted the work of Pollard (2015) in describing the components of a relational ethics approach to decision-making. We have adapted this slightly to better reflect the work of therapists:

Mutual respect:	Holding respect for the client and a sense of responsibility to them
Engagement:	The establishment of a relationship
Embodied knowledge:	Truly understanding the client's needs, preferences and values to guide and orientate decision-making processes (a shared narrative)
Environment:	Understanding the context of the client's social environment (taking account of the client's needs, values, family, community and history)
Uncertainty:	Uncertainties and difficulties in decision-making due to value-based demands

(Pollard, 2015)

Pollard's broad parameters for relational ethics are helpful in that they describe key principles within which we can create an environment for relational ethics to be held centrally in our work. That is: that we *respect* our clients (and their autonomy); we focus on developing, sustaining and exploring the *relationship*; we pay full attention to the *client's perception* of themselves, their needs and what they are looking for in therapy (rather than simply applying our own approach regardless); we see the client in the *context* of their lives (which is critical in taking a position of social justice), and acknowledging the intersectionality in experiences of our clients; and that we hold *multiple truths* in relation to decision-making, in a shared collaborative process with our clients.

Finlay (2019) outlines five important areas of work that speak to relational ethics: *creating an ethical space* (including first meetings and contracting); *boundarying* (creating and agreeing the boundaries for the relationship); *holding* (the holding of the client's story, experiences and needs in focus); *containing* (holding the frame of the relationship in its professional context); and *ending* (acknowledging the diversity of ways endings might occur, and respecting the client's choices in this process). With respect to the establishment of the relationship, key to relational ethics, Finlay uses the acronym of 'therapeutic SPACE':

- *'Supportiveness* stands for the sensitive, compassionate, caring way of being therapists embrace when offering an emotional scaffold for clients to help with their well-being, resilience, and recovery.
- *Playfulness* involves lightness; warm spontaneity, gentle smiles, teasing and humour can all offer an antidote to heavy intensity and shame.
- *Acceptance* helps a client feel seen, validated and not criticised.
- *Curiosity* shows the therapist cares and wants to understand the client better. Together, client and therapist go exploring to make sense of experience.
- *Empathy* concerns being responsively attuned, where therapists sense and feel into their clients' worlds.'

(Finlay, 2019, p. 61)

What is beginning to emerge as we unpack the concept of relational ethics is that it demands a way of thinking, doing, and being. It goes beyond important parameters we might all be familiar with in our work, such as contracting, holding boundaries, and the more general management of sessions. Rather, while these are essential in the creation of a safe therapeutic space, it is how we achieve these and the client's part in co-constructing as many of these ways of being as possible, that enables us to work ethically in a relational, rather than procedural way.

A way of thinking

As we have explored through this chapter, and this book so far, relational ethics demands a different way of thinking with respect to our perception of ethics in our work. It requires that we engage with ethics in a lived way, rather than seeing it simply as a list of rules – or do's and don't's – prescribed in a document that we might have a vague recollection of signing up to at some point in the past. Rather than seeing ethics as a set of concepts or ideas that someone else has created and imposed on us, we need to think about our own relationship to ethics and how we live and breathe our ethical position in life, shaped and influenced by our values, morals, and beliefs. In short, to truly work from a relationally ethical position we need to cease seeing ethics as 'the other', making it about us and who we are as practitioners, as demonstrated in our wider professional actions, as well as in our direct therapeutic work with individuals, couples, groups, or communities.

A way of doing

Having challenged ourselves in terms of how we think about ethics, we then need to integrate that into our work and practice. This, of course, like all therapy begins before the client ever walks into the room or logs in online. The doing of relational ethics demands action and agency that will shape the position we take in the interface with the world. This might take many forms, and some examples are suggested below:

- How do we speak of our work and ourselves online, perhaps through our websites, blogs or on social media?
- How do we speak of our expertise and experiences? Can any one therapist really be an expert on all presenting issues?.
- How do we engage with our clients from the point of first enquiry, to the final contact – and thereafter?
- How do we undertake our contracting process: a matter of passing on information, or an opportunity to talk about how we and the client together might begin to shape the nature of our work (beyond those aspects that might be givens)?
- How do we engage with our clients' stories and, specifically, how we respect and hold the diversity of their experience and worldview? As Khan (2023) says, how do we work *within* diversity rather than *with* it?
- How do we make decisions about what approach should be taken in therapy – do we deliver person-centred therapy, for example, to all our clients because of our belief in its efficacy?
- How do we bring agility to our thinking and work to ensure we meet our clients' changing needs?
- How do we check that things are going to plan and the client's needs are being met.
- How do we know what we are doing is working at all?
- How do we actively share the power of decision-making throughout the process, through to the very end?

Relational ethics demands a particular way of doing our work, underpinned by how we think about our work.

A way of being (and feeling)

Finally, if we are thinking differently about ethics and, in turn, working to do our work differently, both ultimately demand a way of being and feeling about ourselves that supports the development with the client of a shared narrative. We often go to our supervisors, or our colleagues, in the face of a particular challenge that has emerged, with the question, 'What should I do about this/respond to this?'. Perhaps the first question might be to our clients, asking through curiosity and inquisitiveness 'What could we do about this?' Other than relatively few areas of practice where there is an external given, e.g., prevention of terrorism and, in many agencies, safeguarding and child protection, pretty much everything else that happens in the therapeutic encounter is co-constructed between client and therapist. Top-level ethics may determine certain actions and behaviours that would fall outside of ethical therapy, but the navigation and nuance of the therapeutic process is a creative, subtle meeting that is a dynamic and shifting process (even though, at times, it might feel stuck).

To work within a relational ethics frame requires two particular ways of being: a) holding self in a professional frame, mindful of the parameters that keep therapy safe; and b) giving away aspects of self that hold an imbalance of power, preventing the client from truly being present in a way that moves towards equality. These might seem in some ways to be contradictory positions, but in essence they are confluent processes that intertwine. The therapist's way of being is critical here, so that while they remain present in the relationship, the client can be fully present too without that being experienced by the therapist as difficult or challenging.

Much like our personal relationships, the most fulfilling experiences are perhaps those where the way of being inside the relationship is an equal and collaborative experience; where that way of being is co-produced through a process of dialogue, negotiation, compromise, and agreement. This is where we begin to take the concept of relational ethics from a principle to an action.

Reflect on your own approach to ethics from a *thinking, doing,* and *being* perspective: what is your own approach to ethics and what do you do already that you would consider to be an example of relational ethics? Are there some immediate things you might be able to develop to help you adapt to a relational ethics position?

Relational ethics in action

The 'how to' of relational ethics when viewed from an academic or 'in principle' position can appear quite hard to grasp; a bit like trying to catch hold of a wisp of smoke – we know it is there but when we reach out it simply drifts out of the way. Whereas in fact, if we really distil all of this down to a core essence, relational ethics is to do with making decisions about actions and responses in the context of the relationship. As Pollard (2015, p. 364) writes,

> The fundamental nature of relational ethics is that ethical commitment, agency, and responsibility for self and to the other arises out of concrete situations which invariably involve relations between two or more people and affect two or more people. Within this relationship exists embodied selves that are interdependent and connected.

As therapists, we are well-trained to form, develop, sustain, make sense of, and carefully end, relationships. This is what we do – without relationships, we are nothing. Our work happens in relationships, because of relationships and through relationships. We might conceptualise relationships, or indeed be within those relationships slightly differently depending on our training and preferred model(s) of practice, but whether we are humanistically, psychodynamically, cognitive-behaviourally, integratively, or pluralistically informed, the relationship is the vehicle through which our work takes place.

Let's consider the scenario of Victor.

Victor is a 63-year-old Jewish man who has come to therapy because of a sense of isolation and loneliness following the death of his partner eight years before. He regularly visits his local synagogue and finds great comfort in his faith. His family live some distance away and he only sees them occasionally. He has found the work with Daniel, his therapist, to be of huge importance and has been able to talk about things which even Victor hadn't realised were an issue for him. One area that has been of concern for Victor has been his finances, and he struggles to find enough money on a day-to-day basis. He has completed a form for some financial help and asks Daniel to check it for him. Additionally, whether Daniel would write a letter of support to accompany this application for some financial assistance through the synagogue (the application needs a supporting letter from a 'professional').

This is not an uncommon enquiry in therapy. Often, the therapist is best-informed of the details of a client's situation and therefore might be the best advocate for them. But this might also fall outside of the contract that was agreed for therapy, or might begin to blur boundaries and thus potentially make therapy a less safe place. Is Victor beginning to see Daniel as a friend or more general welfare adviser? Or, if Daniel refuses and holds the strict frame of therapy, could this fracture the trust between Victor and Daniel ('you let me down when I needed something from you').

Daniel, like many therapists, is likely to want to talk this through in supervision and may check the ethics document that he follows to see what he should do. However, in all likelihood, Daniel will not find a definitive answer to his question in his ethical framework. He would like it to say, *Daniel, you should definitely write the letter*, or *Daniel, you should definitely not write the letter* – because, at such times, we demand certainty from our ethical frameworks. Like many therapists, he too will close the ethics document on his computer while muttering something about it being a waste of time and offering no guidance at all. Daniel has been left with the dilemma.

The truth probably is some therapists would write the letter and some would not. There will be external factors that may influence that decision, including: organisational policy; modality; personal preference, and beliefs about therapy, for example. However, relational ethics would require Daniel to think about this dilemma differently and, in doing so, position himself differently to the problem. It would demand that Daniel looks back into the relationship with Victor, rather than only looking for an answer outside of it. That he not only looks back into the relationship with Victor, but he talks through the dilemma with Victor, to make him an equal participant in the decision-making process.

This dialogue in and of itself is therapeutic, in that it truly communicates to Victor that he matters in the relationship and his perspectives are important and, in the light of Victor feeling isolated and invisible, he becomes visible again. Together, they decide on the best course of action and together, they decide whether Daniel is the best person to write this letter. This becomes the ethical narrative that Victor and Daniel share between them, that informs their work and further sustains their relationship. This level of ethical reflexivity that Daniel needs to engage in, and share with Victor, is a central tenet of relational ethics, which we will now discuss in the next chapter.

References

Cooper, M. & McLeod, J. (2011). *Pluralistic Counselling and Psychotherapy.* 1st edn. Sage.

Danchev, D. & Ross, A. (2013). *Research Ethics for Counsellors, Nurses and Social Workers.* 1st edn. Sage.

Finlay, L. (2019). *Practical Ethics in Counselling and Psychotherapy.* 1st edn. Sage.

Gabriel, L. & Casemore, R. (2009). *Relational Ethics in Practice.* 1st edn. Taylor & Francis.

Jenkins, P. (2017). *Professional Practice in Counselling and Psychotherapy.* 1st edn. Sage.

Khan, M. (2023). *Working Within Diversity: A Reflective Guide to Anti-Oppressive Practice in Counselling and Therapy.* Jessica Kingsley Publishers.

Pollard, C.L. (2015). What Is the Right Thing to Do: Use of a Relational Ethic Framework to Guide Clinical Decision-*Making International Journal of Caring Sciences,* May–August, 8(2), p. 362.

Proctor, G. (2014). *Values and Ethics in Counselling and Psychotherapy.* 1st edn. Sage.

Tomaselli, G., Buttigieg, S.C., Rosano, A., Cassar, M., & Grima, G. (2020). Person-Centered Care from a Relational Ethics Perspective for the Delivery of High Quality and Safe Healthcare: A Scoping Review. *Front Public Health,* Mar 6. doi: 10.3389/fpubh.2020.00044.

Chapter 4

Reflexive ethical practice

Introduction

In this chapter, we aim to inspire readers to engage, explore, and innovate their own approach to ethics in action through the spirit of acknowledgement and experimentation. By *acknowledgement,* we ask you to adopt open-minded, exploratory approaches to engaging with this text, as well as your exploration of myriad ways and means of ethical being and meaning-making in complex and nuanced counselling or mental health contexts. When we use the term *experimentation,* we invite you to bring your creative and courageous questing mindsets to making sense of your ways of being ethical in navigating helping work and relationships.

So how do we go about understanding, refining, and maintaining our ethical ways of being in our counselling or mental health practice? The creation and continual finessing of informed and experiential approaches to our ethical practice is a never-ending and lifelong process. That said, it is a process of learning and development that gathers pace and depth over time and through lived experience, as we build resources to help with benchmarking and building our new insights and understanding. Benefits accumulate across years and contribute to our expanding knowledge, skills, abilities, and our way of being, not only in a therapeutic context but in our life and lived experiences and contexts. Inevitably for practitioners, this process begins in advance of training, in the preparation for and anticipation of the programme or course ahead. Insights, understandings and meaning-making continuously evolve during lived experience of a practitioner training programme. Such iterative and organic growth is informed and enriched by lived life experiences, our learning and education, and our exposure to diverse cultures and communities.

In this chapter we consider how practitioners can build on their reflexive ways of being and relating in day-to-day work. Importantly,

DOI: 10.4324/9781003354970-4

we endeavour to help practitioners build their own ethical practice benchmarking process and framework for their helping work through developing a *pluralistic relational ethics toolkit*. Finally, we consider aspects of philosophical and pragmatic relational ethics, informed by contributors in Chapter 2.

Training, CPD and ongoing growth: cultivating experiential and reflexive ways of being and working

The following sections explore aspects and features of the helping landscape that feed into building a lifelong approach to relational ethics. We outline an approach that embeds congruent, authentic, and compassionate relating, living, and working. We reflect on core practitioner training, continuing professional development (CPD) and personal growth, scope of practice, and competencies in the counselling professions and supervisory consultation. In the process we challenge some of the 'received wisdom' of the helping professions.

As people enter training for helping and counselling professions, inevitable discombobulation and development rapidly evolve. Competencies and confidence grow incrementally through taught content and associated practicum and placement experiences, and importantly, with their peers, trainees build a group with whom they can swap opinions and provide co-consultancy as they grow their knowledge, skills, and abilities. For some trainees their fellow learners will become lifelong professional and personal companions, lending further supporting with navigation of day-to-day practice across a practitioner's working lifetime.

Fostering ongoing learning occurs through diverse channels. Trainees spend time in supervisory contexts, both within and outside of their core training. During and beyond core training, practitioners engage in continuing professional development (CPD) to enhance and inform their knowledge, skills, and abilities. Additionally, ongoing personal growth occurs as we learn more about ourselves through our therapy and non-therapy relationships and contexts. Being exposed to a training curriculum, seminar content, associated reading, and dialogical processes engaged with during training influences how practitioners engage with their helping work. Whilst core training is expected to provide a good grounding in theory and practice, it can never fully prepare students for post-experience practice. In Chapter 2, one of the contributors suggests that trainees need fewer theories and concepts and more opportunities to learn about ways of being, relating, and working in therapeutic contexts. Such an approach might mitigate anxiety about learning diverse and conflicted theories. Moreover, it provides trainees with opportunities to reflexively consider their practice against a backdrop of theories and concepts that can come alive through lived experience of practising skills, delving into attitudes and values, and deepening understanding of 'who am I' in this work? Likewise, there are ways of extending self and other awareness, and our consideration of implications for practice, through exploration in supported training settings. See Box 4.1 for reflexive prompts. We suggest you consider them as relational ethics prompts that you can consider on your own. Equally, you might find it helpful to reflect on them in a conversational space with a supervisor or colleague. They are also useful for training and CPD contexts.

Box 4.1 Exploring our ways of being with self and others

- Why do I want to become a practitioner?
- What's my motivation?
- Who am I doing it for?
- What value judgements and principles do I bring to my work?
- How might they influence or impact on my work with colleagues and clients?
- What are my personal limitations? Are there any relational limits or presenting issues or clients that I know I might/ would be challenged by?
- Which of my personal qualities or characteristics might hinder my work as a practitioner?
- Are there people I could not work with?
- Are there contexts or practice settings I could not work in?
- In my practice work and therapeutic relationships, who do I see as responsible for what, in the day-to-day therapy work and relational dynamics?

Focussed exploration through reading about therapeutic approaches can provide a helpful overview and prompt interest in further training and development opportunities. Seminal texts on therapeutic modalities can signpost readers to further training. See for example, Mearns, Thorne, and McLeod (2013) and Merry (2002)m who provided exemplar texts for person-centred practice. From a psychodynamic approach, see Jacobs' work (2012), or for a cognitive-behaviourist perspective see Beck (2020), or from an integrative or pluralistic mindset see Cooper and McLeod (2011), Cooper and Dryden (2015), Norcross and Goldfried (2014), or Smith and De La Prida (2021).

Whereas all helping approaches would likely acknowledge the value of a Rogerian informed person-centred approach (PCA) to helping work, not all will uphold the notion that person-centred counselling can sufficiently convey the diverse concepts, cultural practices, and nuanced decision-making necessary for the day-to-day minutiae of client–practitioner work and relating. That said, it would be impossible to prepare a trainee for all eventualities. Nonetheless, as trainers, we must generate opportunities for practitioners to develop their skills, knowledge, and abilities to form a relational ethics toolkit. Authentically valuing and prioritising client agency, dialogue, and collaboration with the therapist typifies a pluralistic approach to therapy work.

Training approaches informed by pluralism are usually underpinned by values and virtues that prize inclusive and socially just practice. Whilst all approaches would likely subscribe to elements of principle ethics and, in particular, beneficence (*for the good of the client*) and non-maleficence (*do no harm to the client*), differences exist in the nuanced ways in which the course's modality influences training content on therapeutic relationships and processes. To equip and prepare trainees for the workplace or for private practice, ideally, courses will provide opportunities to consider administration of routine outcome measures (ROMs).

Gathering data through ROMs can be done in a person-centred and relational way and can provide a collaborative means for client and therapist to review how therapy is progressing. For service providers, evidence gathered through ROMs is important for bidding and commissioning purposes. Significantly, some of the key measures currently in use – in particular ReQOL (Reclaiming Quality of Life measure) – were co-produced and developed in consultation with clients and patients. Training programmes and associated placement contexts can support trainees to explore and consider how best to embed appropriate measures and evaluation into day-to-day practice.

Each training course's theoretical underpinnings will bring perceptions, perspectives, and practices, as well as concepts, beliefs, and associated values to influence the trainee practitioner. Pluralistic approaches to practitioner training and education are a recent development in the counselling and therapy fields, led by the work of both McLeod and Cooper (2011). A pluralistic approach as presented in the literature indicates both a *mindset* (Smith et al., 2021) and a *pragmatic framework* for practice (see for example, Cooper and McLeod, 2007, 2011; Smith & De La Prida, 2021; Cooper & Dryden, 2016). Notably, a pluralistic mindset and training, acknowledges challenges prompted by social, political, and economic injustices.

Post-training, ongoing replenishment, of both a personal and professional nature, is an important feature of professional helping work. Post-experience CPD events are widely available, and with the recent increase in the availability of online events, it makes accessible and affordable workshops and training available on a global scale. Whilst many have written about counsellor education and development, there is limited research on or critique of training delivery and impact. We include a textbook on the ethics of training in this Routledge *Ethics in Action* series.

Reading for relaxation, reparation, and reflexivity

In relation to our ongoing personal, relational, and professional development, engaging with publications that propose edgy or innovative ways of thinking and working can be an excellent way of challenging and extending our knowledge and understanding. To explore a non-medicalised approach to mental health work, Sanders and Tolan's 2023 book *People Not Pathology: Freeing Therapy from the Medical Model* offers an alternative psychosocial and relational perspective that provides accessible and compelling examples of non-pathologising interventions and services in the UK. There are increasing numbers of publications on ethics, social justice, decolonisation, anti-oppressive practice, and the intersections of injustices. The following suggestions in Box 4.2 are just a few of the textbooks we would suggest are valuable resources for contemporary practice.

Box 4.2 Suggested reading

Dwight Turner (2023) – *The Psychology of Supremacy: Imperium; The Intersections of Privilege and Otherness in Counselling and Psychotherapy: Mockingbird.* Routledge.

Myira Khan (2023) – *Working Within Diversity: A Reflective Guide to Anti-Oppressive Practice in Counselling and Psychotherapy.* Jessica Kingsley Publishers.

Colin Lago and Divine Charura (2022) – edited textbook, *Black Identities and White Therapies: Race, Respect and Diversity.* PCCS Books.

Laura Winter and Divine Charura (2023, October) – edited textbook, *The Handbook of Social Justice in Psychological Therapies: Power, Politics and Change.* Sage.

Linda Finlay (2021) – *Practical Ethics in Counselling and Psychotherapy: A Relational Approach.* Sage.

Lynne Gabriel and Roger Casemore (2009) – edited textbook, *Relational Ethics in Practice: Narratives from Counselling and Psychotherapy.* Routledge.

Lynne Gabriel (2005) – *Speaking the Unspeakable: The Ethics of Dual Relationships in Counselling and Psychotherapy.* Routledge.

Gillian Proctor (2014) – *Values & Ethics in Counselling and Psychotherapy.* Sage.

Gillian Proctor (2017) – *The Dynamics of Power in Counselling and Psychotherapy: Ethics, Politics, and Practice.* PCCS Books.

Andrew Reeves (2015) – *Working with Risk in Counselling and Psychotherapy.* Sage.

Dee Danchev and Alistair Ross (2013) – *Research Ethics for Counsellors, Nurses & Social Workers.* Sage.

Kate Smith and Ani De La Prida (2021) – *The Pluralistic Therapy Primer.* PCCS Books.

Scope of practice and competencies

Current training in counselling and psychotherapy tends to be based on levels of education and theoretical modality, with a proliferation of quality programmes available through universities, colleges, private training institutes and local councils. Unlike practitioner psychologists, or social work and allied health professionals, UK counselling and psychotherapy are not subject to statutory regulation. The implications are that their associated training routes are unregulated. There are pros and cons to being a regulated profession. One advantage of regulation is that public and employer perceptions of professional status are heightened, and credibility accrues around regulated titles such as counselling psychologist or clinical psychologist. Sadly, we have a situation in Great Britain where counselling and psychotherapy are regarded as low down on the professional hierarchy of mental health practitioners.

However, nine UK professional bodies took action to enhance regulator, public and organisational understanding of the value of counselling and psychotherapy. The professional bodies collaborated to map counsellor and psychotherapist training competencies and scope of practice through the SCoPED (*scope of practice and education*) project. Many practitioners and organisations that employ therapists have valued the SCoPED project. Opposition to perceived inequities across the mapping of counselling and psychotherapy was reminiscent of historical splits in these UK professions. Given the value of having a scope of practice for a helping profession – not least in relation to employment and scheduling work programmes – it is hoped that professional bodies can consult with and inform their memberships, and that the field can move forward positively and productively. Critics have regarded SCoPED as a divisive approach that pits counsellor against psychotherapist and generates an unhelpful hierarchical divide, with counselling 'at the bottom of the ladder', generating antipathies between counselling and psychotherapy. Despite a significant minority opposing SCoPED, it received formal approval in early 2023 from the nine professional bodies who collaborated to research and develop the framework that was adopted and implemented by the bodies across 2023 and into 2024.

Arguably, as a clearly articulated and evidence-based competency framework and scope of practice, SCoPED offers a useful framework for employers, commissioners of therapy services, and training providers. Significantly, its development and promotion in the public domain could positively influence members of the public to access counselling or psychotherapy services, in the belief that SCoPED conveys a competent and trained workforce of counsellors and psychotherapists. Importantly, a clear training and registration route for those seeking to work in the helping profession is essential and SCoPED does offer UK employing organisations and other professions an overview of the competencies involved in counselling and psychotherapy roles. It remains to be seen how SCoPED will influence counsellor and psychotherapist employment. Professional bodies and the UK Professional Standards Authority (PSA) have a responsibility to advocate for the value of these professional roles.

As members of the UK helping professions, the existence of non-statutorily regulated occupational roles in counselling and psychotherapy has been a context in which tribal tensions have prevailed. Nonetheless, to advance our profession, we need to manage our human propensities towards tribalism and co-create constructive dialogues to influence the trajectory of a professional landscape that facilitates rather than freezes progress. Opposition, challenge, and critique are important to help inform and shape constructive changes and new directions. What hinders or blocks are toxic and damaging dynamics of internecine conflict; these need to be 'called out'. In this dialogical and discursive process, through recognition of inevitably diverse opinion and valuing of coalescing forces and facts, exists potential for a positive paradigm shift in the UK to embed recognition and acknowledgement of the increasing value of counselling and psychotherapy.

There is increasing interest in the role of the psychological professions as global mental ill-health and distress increases through natural interventions (e.g., disasters and pandemics) and human interventions (e.g., war). Our UK status as non-regulated professionals, subject to accredited voluntary registration through a PSA approved register, could shift with a change of government. Typically, a Labour government is more risk-averse and if they are successful in the next UK elections they will bring a political regime that is more likely to consider statutory regulation of the counselling and psychotherapy professions. Worryingly, this is contingent upon the fickle and fractured nature of UK politics. In the meantime, the development of the profession continues. Notwithstanding the regulatory and SCoPED challenges in the UK, training and preparation for entering the profession as a trained professional is a context through which trainees learn about themselves as a practitioner, and about ways of being in relationship with clients – all important aspects of relational ethics. For frontline practitioners, we suggest embedding pluralistic pragmatic relational ethics into your work to extend your reflexive practice.

Contextualised supervision and consultation

Supervisory or consultative support creates crucial and central relational contexts in which practitioners can process ongoing helping practices and 'benchmark' their work through supportive consultation with their supervisor. Supervision and peer or professional consultation is essential to ongoing personal and professional development and growth. Importantly, it's a great context in which ways of being and relating through a relational ethics prism could be explored reflexively. In the UK, many practitioners are subject to mandatory and life-long supervision. The value of supervision is recognised, with increasing availability of supervisor training programmes and CPD and a growth in supervision research. Core to the supervision process are the parallel relational dimensions and domains, captured well by Hawkins and Shohet's (2012) multimodal approach. From the perspective of ethics in action, a supervisory setting provides an exploratory space in which the supervisor and supervisee can examine the minutiae of day-to-day practice. Ideally, the supervisory relationship is a positive, productive, mutually respectful medium through which a supervisee can enhance their practitioner knowledge, skills, and abilities (Dunnett et al., 2013).

Developing relational reflexivity for ethics in action

Self-awareness and reflexivity

Negotiating tricky relational terrain is never easy or straightforward. Self and other awareness can be a great ally in such challenging musings and relationship negotiations. Growth of self-awareness involves an ability to reflect on oneself and one's practices, and to reflexively integrate insights and learning into our expressions in and through work and relationships. Of central significance is constant self-monitoring; moment by moment self/other observation and tracking of relational content and dynamics. Not of the kind that could be anxiety-invoking, but more a deliberate, mindful, and positive focus on learning more about self, self in relationship(s), and our impact on those we are working with.

Opportunities arise regularly throughout practitioner training and post-experience CPD, for reflexive and rich iterative advancement of knowledge, skills, and abilities. Peer relations, membership of peer support groups in-person and online, and supervision, all contribute to enriching our sense of self as a practitioner and our understanding of how our work sits within the wider counselling and mental health professions. It is important to be able to understand how to navigate the relational dynamics with self and with others, through building self-awareness and reflexivity.

Crafting collaborations and connections with trusted others – people that positively contribute to individual and collective ongoing growth – is core to building valuable networks. Such connections can help us to navigate tricky relational terrain across personal and professional contexts. Fundamentally, mustering friends and others who know and value you, who can laugh and cry with you, who can share human life and experiences with you, and who want to spend time with you, is so precious, and crucial for navigating the complexities of human existence and life. People in the helping and counselling professions are vulnerable to burnout and vicarious trauma. Affording care and compassion to self and others can elicit reciprocal benefit for practitioners' work, and for the recipients of their work and relationships.

Client measures, feedback, and evaluation

Feedback and data from clients' experiences and perceptions of the services they receive provides helpful information that can be used for multiple purposes, including the impact of therapy received. The use of standardised measures in counselling, psychotherapy, psychology, and mental health professions is both a contested and an encouraged area of practice. Whilst it may be essential for service providers or commissioned organisations to gather information on therapy impact and outcomes, there are significant issues to consider in relation to the administration and use of routine outcome measures and the relational ethics of administering forms on a regular basis.

The use of measures provides a counselling or helping service with indicators of therapy impact, through administration of pre- and post-therapy and sessional scales to assess client change or recovery. The concept of recovery is used within medicalised settings such as the UK NHS Talking Therapies for people experiencing anxiety and depression. Humanistic and integrative psychology has long advocated the development of person-centred, non-pathologising or psychosocial ways of perceiving and conceptualising human distress and mental ill-health. This focus has shaped and influenced the development of counselling and psychotherapy.

Other non-medicalised frameworks for human mental health and wellbeing include the *Power, Threat, Meaning* model, developed by clinical psychologists (Johnstone & Boyle, 2018). The bases of non-medicalised, non-pathologising approaches to helping and counselling professions are core values that inform ways of being, meaning-making, relating, and working (Sanders & Tolan, 2023). These include recognition and valuing of inclusivity and acknowledgement of the impact of international colonialism and oppression on therapy theories and practices (Cooper, 2023; Sanders & Tolan, 2023; Smith et al., 2021). Additionally, contemporary developments include recognition of the diverse and complex power dynamics within healthcare, psychological therapies, and mental healthcare contexts (Finlay, 2019; Proctor, 2017).

Oddly missing from routine outcome measure (ROM) development and administration, are client voices and perspectives. There are some exceptions, including the development of ReQOL (reclaiming quality of life) (Grundy et al. 2019), where patients and clients were key contributors to the development of the measure. This is uncommon at the time of writing and an area of practice that requires further investigation and collaborative research that includes clients, patients, and others with lived experiences of accessing counselling and mental health services.

Pragmatic resources

To support helping practitioners organise and coordinate their values, knowledge, concepts, and potential responses to day-to-day practice challenges, the following sections include accessible resources for creating and sustaining an ethics in practice 'toolkit' or portfolio. Such resources are enlivened through conversation, consideration, and collaboration. They demand dialogue, with self, with others through peer and supervisory contexts, and importantly, with clients. Additionally, there is significant value in research conversations with those involved in all aspects of therapy provision, to prompt exploration and processing of client–therapist relational dynamics. There is also a rich range of relational and behavioural resources offered in Chapters 3 and 5.

Ethical decision-making models and approaches

Professional bodies usually offer a range of ethical decision-making (EDM) resources for practitioner members. For example, the British Association for Counselling & Psychotherapy (BACP) publishes multiple resources, including an ethical decision-making model developed by Gabriel (BACP, 2021, GPiA044) – see Figures 4.1 and 4.2, and

Figure 4.1 A model and mindset for creating relational ethics in practice

Table 4.1 below. The American Counseling Association (ACA) and the American Psychological Association (APA) also publish a wide range of EDMs and resources.

Decision-making models are not definitive tools, but simply aides, and it is the role of the practitioner, in dialogue with themselves and

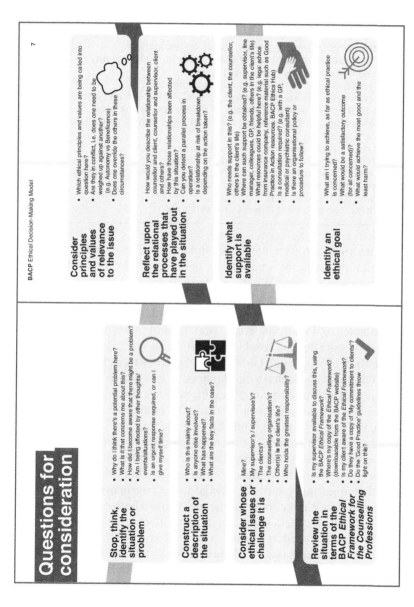

Figure 4.2 Questions to support ethical decision-making

Table 4.1 Actions for ethics in practice

Step	Practitioner Actions
1	Stop, think, identify the situation or problem
2	Construct a description of the situation, including any complicating contextual features
3	Consider *whose ethical issue or challenge it is?*
4	Review the situation in terms of BACP *Ethical Framework*
5	Identify principles and values of relevance to the issue
6	Reflect on relational processes that have played out in the situation
7	Identify what support is available
8	Identify an ethical goal and way forward
9	Consider possible courses of action to achieve the ethical goal
10	Implement your chosen course of action
11	Evaluate the outcome
12	Check for personal impact and self-care

colleagues (including trainers and supervisors) to identify an approach that offers a most appropriate decision or way forward in any significant risk situation. What we offer here are best viewed as pragmatic tools to support practitioner meaning-making throughout the multiple dimensions and minutiae of day-to-day practice; including those complex and daunting events that most of us encounter at some point in our working and lived life experiences.

The notion of 'questing' (Gabriel, 2016) offers a metaphor to inform ethical relational decisions in our day-to-day practice, as well as within the context of urgent and complex ethical issues. Imagine that, when questing, we are making meaning through collaborative engagement with clients and colleagues, and through reading and engaging with books and research papers, in pursuit of insights and understandings. This might also involve delving into relevant reports or studies from allied professions or disciplines, to inform our thinking. There is no doubt that questing requires courage and congruence to navigate what can be messy and conflicted therapy work. The use of intentional questing alongside other creative practice tools and tactics, such as the concepts 'boundary riders', 'ethics warriors', and 'sentinels' (Gabriel, 2005; 2009; 2016), can assist with navigating pathways through tricky relational terrain. Whether an ethical issue arises in the context of a guided training scenario or through the actual lived experience of a practice setting, decisions must be made about day-to-day ethics in practice.

The ethical decision-making model (EDM) depicted in the figures above (BACP, 2018) offers a multidimensional, pluralistic approach to decision-making in ethical practice and is one of many models available to practitioners. In the UK and US, practitioners can access EDMs through their professional bodies. A recent review from Johnson et al. (2022) provides a helpful overview of Pacific Rim approaches. They reviewed the theoretical bases of the EDMs and offer an accessible taxonomy for practitioner-readers seeking guidance on which model to use. However, they need to be brought into the 21st century, critiqued for relevance across diverse ethnicities, and made widely available for integration into practice.

Caring and compassionate mindsets and approaches

Within an educational context, Nell Noddings posited an *ethic of care*, influenced by educational and feminist concepts and informed by her ideas about good maternal care. What Noddings terms 'situation ethics' (Noddings, 1995: 9) is an ethic of care that regards justice as a key aim, with an emphasis on creating a caring environment to facilitate compassionate care. An approach that recognises that intractable individual differences do occur, it avoids a general or universal claim to resolution. This resonates with a metamodern mindset and approach to relationships. From this position, a practitioner acknowledges that irreconcilable forces operate in relation to clients' presenting issues and they will work in partnership with the client to negotiate a route through the client's issues.

As briefly noted earlier, an important recent development in counselling and clinical psychology saw the introduction of the *Power, Threat, Meaning* (PTM) framework. Conceptualised by Lucy Johnstone and Mary Boyle (Johnstone and Boyle, 2018), PTM offers an alternative, relational approach to conceptualising mental distress. Johnstone and Boyle acknowledge the multilayered role of power in the emergence of distress and identified links between perception of threats and threat responses. They argue that meaning-making, and the building of explanatory narratives, is not a biological process but one of mentalisation. They challenge injustices inherent in medicalised perspectives on mental health and call to action the psychological therapies professions to challenge inequities and social injustices. Such a psychosocial and cultural approach resonates with core elements of humanistic psychology (including Rogers' core conditions) and echoes the pluralistic movement's focus on social justice, epistemic injustices (including discrimination of multiple kinds and denial of people's realities and lived experiences), valuing of individual and community-based social, cultural, and relational values, and recognition of the importance of inclusivity.

The PTM framework offers an important alternative to the medical model of mental ill-health, as defined in the DSM-5 classification and the ICD-11, and is beginning to gain ground with many practitioner psychologists and psychiatrists, as community mental health adopts a person-centred and co-produced focus and ways of working. Importantly, it places the client central to a person-centred endeavour, whilst also recognising the pluralistic nature and complexities of cultural, social, and political heritages, and their potential impact upon therapy work and relationships.

Towards pluralistic relational ethics

The centrality of relationship and relational lenses was evident in the Chapter 2 research conversations with contributors. The importance of our relationships with self and with others is clearly paramount. In parallel, in a therapy context, we have our own and clients' intersecting contexts including families, partners, friendships, colleagues, organisations, systems, and communities. Additionally, we have local, national, and global politics and economics to factor in. Importantly, our lived internal intrapersonal dialogues are as significant as external interpersonal contexts and dynamics. Through accruing life and lived experiences, and engagement in the learning and knowledge opportunities of practitioner training, these become important and complex dimensions to factor into our work and ways of being – both in the world and in our counselling or mental health work.

Building our approach to relational ethics through embracing internal and external dimensions and by acknowledging the diversity and plurality of influences and experiences, creates and acknowledges complexity alongside fertile relational seams for exploration and new understanding. Such a pluralistic perspective provides a way forward for contemporary approaches to relational ethics and offers future-proofing, as it provides a flexible framework that can adjust to theoretical, clinical, and societal changes. Embedding collaborative, social justice-informed pluralistic mindsets into the formation of *pluralistic relational ethics* offers a multidimensional, vibrant, reflexive, and inclusive way of considering ethics. And fundamentally, to signpost ways of being in the world and with others.

The phenomenon of a constantly evolving relational ethic dominates. We are constantly vibrating and responding to the minutiae of relational interactions and interconnectedness. For thousands of years, ethical thinking has been founded on predominantly white, westernised male thinking. These tenets that underpin much of the ethics, psychology, and counselling theories require challenging and bringing into the 21st century. We need new concepts and approaches for ethics as a relational framework for life and relationships in a diverse world. Guides that are fit for purpose are required.

The central tenet of pluralistic relational ethics espoused here is the capacity to sustain oneself through diversity, complexity, and uncertainty. The crux of the matter is the necessity for moment-by-moment reflexive ethical decision-making; essentially, evolving a way of being that emerges and matures over time. Ideally, practitioner training supports trainees to build reflexivity, resilience, and responsibility to be able to track relational minutiae and to chart ways through the inevitable and multiple types of practice challenges.

Adopting an approach that embraces humility and avoids power posturing (Bergum & Dossetor, 2005), can generate opportunities to work collaboratively with clients to bring about meaningful and impactful processes of change. A pluralistic mindset sees people as interdependent and interconnected. People co-produce through relationships and relational interactions, which are often occurring in relation to place-based projects, such as the recent UK development of community mental health hubs. Traditional biomedical ethics and the notions of autonomy, equality, and the self as an independent entity are questionable in relation to diverse cultural and racial groups. The norms of equity and justice, and the benchmark of anti-oppressive responsibility, preside within the pluralistic relationship. The ethical imperative becomes that of an embodied other in relational dialogue and interaction with the 'other' of the therapist (Bergum & Dossetor, 2005) – and extended to 'others' in the context of group, family, or systems work. This is a more fluid conception of relationship interactions that acknowledges human luminosity, liminal transitions, and questing through uncharted territory. The challenge exists in navigating this relational terrain, for which there are no clear-cut guidance templates, only places and spaces for courageous and compassionate exploration. We become the instrument and medium through which we cultivate our relational ethics.

References

BACP (2018). *Ethical Framework for the Counselling Professions*. BACP.

BACP (2021). *Good Practice in Action GPiA044: Ethical Decision-making in the Context of the Counselling Professions*. BACP.

Beck, J.S. (2020). *Cognitive Behavior Therapy: Basics and Beyond*. Guilford Press.

Bergum, V. & Dossetor, J. (2005). *Relational Ethics. The Full Meaning of Respect*. University Publishing Group.

Cooper, M. (2023). *Psychology at the Heart of Social Change: Developing a Progressive Vision for Society*. Policy Press.

Cooper, M. & Dryden, W. (2015). *The Handbook of Pluralistic Counselling and Psychotherapy*. Sage.

Cooper, M. & McLeod, J. (2011). *Pluralistic Counselling and Psychotherapy*. Sage.

Dunnett, A., Jesper, C., O'Donnell, M., & Vallance, K. (2013). *Getting the Most from Supervision: A Guide for Counsellors and Psychotherapists*. Palgrave.

Finlay, L. (2019). *Practical Ethics in Counselling and Psychotherapy: A Relational Approach*. Sage.

Gabriel, L. (2005). *Speaking the Unspeakable: The Ethics of Dual Relationships in Counselling and Psychotherapy*. Routledge.

Gabriel, L. & Casemore, R. (2009). Eds. *Relational Ethics in Practice: Narratives from Counselling and Psychotherapy*. Routledge.

Gabriel, L. (2016). Ethics in Pluralistic Counselling and Psychotherapy. In Cooper, M., & Dryden, W. (eds) *Handbook of Pluralistic Counselling and Psychotherapy*, pp. 300–313. Sage.

Grundy, A., Keetharuth, A.D., Barber, R. et al. (2019). Public Involvement in Health Outcomes Research: Lessons Learnt from the Development of the Recovering Quality of Life (ReQoL) Measures. *Health Qual Life Outcomes* 17(60). doi:10.1186/s12955-019-1123-z

Hawkins, P. & Shohet, R. (2012) *Supervision in the Helping Professions*. McGraw-Hill Education (UK).

Jacobs, M. (2012). *The Presenting Past: The Core of Psychodynamic Counselling and Therapy*. Open University Press.

Johnson, M.K., Weeks, S.N., Peacock, G.G., & Rodriguez, M.M.D. (2022). Ethical Decision-Making Models: A Taxonomy of Models and Review of Issues. *Ethics & Behavior*, 32(3), 195–210. doi:10.1080/10508422.2021.1913593.

Johnstone, L. & Boyle, M. (2018). The Power Threat Meaning Framework: An Alternative Nondiagnostic Conceptual System. *Journal of Humanistic Psychology*, 1–18. doi:10.1177/0022167818793289

Mearns, D., Thorne, B., & McLeod, J. (2013). *Person-Centred Counselling in Action*. Sage.

Merry, T. (2002). *Learning and Being in Person-Centred Counselling*. PCCS Books.

Noddings, N. (1995). Caring. In *Justice and Care: Essential Readings in Feminist Ethics*. Ed., Virginia Held. Routledge.

Norcross, J. & Goldfried, M.R. (2014). *Handbook of Psychotherapy Integration*. Oxford Academic.

Proctor, G. (2017) *The Dynamics of Power in Counselling and Psychotherapy: Ethics, Politics and Practice* (2nd edn). PCCS Books.

Sanders, P. & Tolan, J. (2023). *People Not Pathology: Freeing Therapy from the Medical Model*. PCCS Books.

Smith, K. & De La Prida, A. (2021). *The Pluralistic Therapy Primer: A Concise Introduction*. PCCS Books.

Smith, K., McLeod, J., Blunden, N., Cooper, M., Gabriel, L., Kupfer, C., McLeod, J., Murphie, M-C., Oddli, H.W., Thurston, M. & Winter, L.A. (2021). A Pluralistic Perspective on Research in Psychotherapy: Harnessing Passion, Difference and Dialogue to Promote Justice and Relevance. *Frontiers of Psychology,* vol. 12. |doi:10.3389/fpsyg.2021.742676

Chapter 5

Building an ethics in action toolkit

Here we present a pluralistic, relational approach to ethics in action. We will provide a synthesised toolkit for how practitioners can integrate relational ethics into their work, drawing on the perspectives outlined in Chapter 2; a toolkit for working ethically across multiple contexts and presenting issues, including how such a 'toolkit' might be translated into a multidisciplinary context, as well as adapted for other allied professionals.

Introducing relational ethics in action

In previous chapters, we have talked about the importance of working ethically in a general sense, and the particular value a relational ethics approach in our work can bring to the therapeutic process. We have argued that top-level ethics offer important parameters to our work, but that often therapists struggle to bridge top-level ethics to the detail of their work, linking ethics to practice. Often, therapists experience top-level ethics as attending to broader brush concepts and ideas – and additionally struggle to embed such ethical thinking in a way that is consistent with the micro aspects of the therapeutic relationship.

In this context we might ask why therapists wouldn't naturally be using a relational approach to ethics already; after all, what is there not to like? Relational ethics:

*   Privileges the therapeutic relationship as the primary vehicle through which ethically informed decisions are made.
*   Respects the autonomy and voice of the client in decision-making.
*   Proactively supports the process of therapeutic collaboration.
*   Communicates to the client the therapist's intention of transparently working through – with the client – issues that emerge.

DOI: 10.4324/9781003354970-5

- Strengthens the therapeutic relationship and brings with it the potential for relational depth.
- Is sufficiently flexible to honour that therapists work from different modalities, or indeed a pluralistic position, and can orientate the discourse around ethics according to the modality used, or the plan for therapy.
- Can further support the development of goals (if consistent with the therapist's modality), or further honour the client's narrative about their preferences for therapy.
- Brings ethics into the 'real world' of therapy and bridges top-level ethics with the particular nuances of the therapeutic process.

What further advantages to you see in your own work from embedding a relational approach to ethics, drawing on your own client experiences. How have you sought to solve issues in the past?

Having outlined the many benefits to the therapeutic and decision-making process of relational ethics, there may be some challenges for therapists to find a starting point for integrating this approach into their work. These might include:

- Client-centred focus
- Training experiences around ethics
- Theoretical orientation
- Other personal biases
- Particular ethical challenges
- Pressures beyond the relationship
- Cultural and contextual differences
- Fear of confrontation
- Supervisory support
- Development in ethics thinking

Client-centred focus

By 'client-centred focus' we do not mean client-centred therapy, but rather an over-preoccupation on the process of the client at the expense of a focus on the relationship and subsequent dynamics. This may seem a counter-intuitive starting point, given that we have argued relational ethics sit at the heart of the relationship in therapy. However, there are occasions where we can be so consumed by the needs of the clients that we fail to notice power dynamics and other relational issues that might be at play in the relationship itself. There may be times when a relational dynamic is more pressing to attend to than the experience of the client in that moment, which is where relational ethics really becomes a tour-de-force.

> How do you hold the balance between client process and relational dynamic in considering your work with clients?

Training experiences around ethics

Most training programmes in the UK for therapists include training around ethics. These often relate to key processes in ethical decision-making, as well as an important familiarisation of the ethics of some of the professional associations, which students may be members of. What is less certain, however, is how much attention is paid to what is meant by relational ethics and, specifically, *how* therapists might draw on relational ethics in the therapeutic process itself. This is a discrete skill in that while it does draw on the key therapy skills and management of boundaries, etc., the negotiation with a client around key ethical considerations that emerge during the work might sometimes fall beyond a therapist's confidence.

> How did your core training enable you to work effectively with ethics in practice, and were there other aspects you might have wanted to have been included? What additional steps could you take to further support your confidence in ethical decision-making?

Theoretical orientation

While we have argued above that relational ethics can be segued into different modalities and approaches to work, there is a process of translation that must be navigated for this to be successful. That is, while the principles of relational ethics would be applicable to all therapeutic approaches, given that all therapy is bound to the process of the relationship, *how* the therapist understands and works with that relationship will vary across the primary therapy paradigms, e.g., humanistic, psychodynamic, cognitive-behavioural, and integrative / pluralistic. Therefore, therapists need to think about how they would work within the relationship to attend to ethical issues as they emerge, that remains consistent with, and supportive of, the wider therapeutic process.

> How does your modality of practice shape and inform how you engage with your own ethical thinking, and in ethical decision-making with your clients?

Other personal biases

Self-awareness sits at the heart of relationship ethics, so that ethical decision-making processes that sit within the therapeutic relationship can be considered through a relational lens. As therapists, we bring our biases and stereotyped views of the world as much as anyone else might. What is important, is that we consider these in our reflexive position so that we bring as much from the 'unknown' into the known. It is less that we *should* hold particular views of the world, but rather, we are *aware* of the views we do hold to ensure they are not acted out. The impact and experience of the relationship with the client will be critically important also; some modalities might frame this as the transferential and countertransferential dynamics that sit within all relationships. Whatever our own description of these processes, they undoubtedly exist and need attending to.

> What mechanisms do you draw on to reflect on your own world-view, and how does your own cultural positioning shape your relationship with ethics in practice?

Particular ethical challenges

There may be some ethical challenges that provoke anxiety in therapists, particularly in working with clients in a collaborative way. These often relate to points at which the therapist perceives a relational boundary might be compromised. Examples of this might include: risk; attraction; financial uncertainties around the therapy itself; and other points of disclosure where the therapist believes a contractual transgression may or has occurred. Points at which the therapist experiences feelings of anxiety in bringing the issue back to the client can contribute to a move away from a relationally ethical position.

> Are there ethical situations that you encounter more than others? How do you manage the impact on you of making ethical decisions?

Pressures beyond the relationship

Likewise, there may be issues that sit beyond the immediacy of the relationship itself, or the specific contract, that can feel difficult to talk about with clients. Examples of such situations may include: a period of absence of the therapist due to extended breaks; illness; organisational expectations (including changes in organisational expectations); and other points where the contract needs to be varied or re-negotiated.

> How do you hold the interface between what happens inside the therapeutic relationship and those factors that are outside of the process but seem to impinge on it?

Cultural and contextual differences

Working with diversity (and *within* diversity; Khan, 2023) in the therapeutic relationship requires a level of reflexivity by practitioners in considering a multitude of important areas, including: power; social injustice; privilege; and how power is then positioned, held, and navigated in the relational process. It can therefore be a particular challenge for therapists to consider how to engage with ethical dilemmas or challenges in the relationship while also respecting difference. The fear is that inadvertently, by taking ethical positions (which may be perceived to be rooted in, and informed by, power), the client's autonomy is undermined, rather than respected (Proctor, 2014).

Thinking of Khan's (2023) helpful challenge for therapists to think about working within, rather than with, diversity, how do you navigate ethical challenges while respecting the difference that sits between you and your client?

Fear of confrontation

We choose the word 'confrontation' here deliberately, as the perception is that any dialogue that might hold within it different perspectives might be confrontational, i.e., likely to end in disagreement or a fracture in the relationship. We would argue, however, that navigating ethical dilemmas can be far from relational and instead facilitate insight, growth, and relational depth.

Confrontation: how do you deal with points of disagreement or difference in thinking in a way that supports the therapeutic process?

Supervisory support

A key aspect of drawing on the principles of working with relational ethics is that this is also informed by that same process in supervision. Often, therapists can think of supervision more akin to case management – a systematic reviewing of a caseload – particularly when hugely busy and under the pressure of a waiting list. Or, perhaps through the demands from the working context. We have both been involved in supervising schools' counselling, for example, which often brings with it regular safeguarding concerns. What is important in supporting a relational ethics position, therefore, is that the groundwork for taking this back into the therapeutic relationship needs to be addressed in supervision. A positive paralleling of a process: if we can find our way of making some sense of what relational ethics means to us in supervision, then we can begin to bridge that more effectively into our client work.

How do you talk about relational ethics with your supervisor, and how does that then bridge back into and inform your practice?

Development in ethics thinking

Finally, of course, is that ethics itself is not a static entity. Rather, it is a shifting, changing, dynamic process that moves with social conventions, diverse influences and perspectives, changing social norms, values and moral positions, and the changing demands of practice. Some can often feel overwhelmed by the uncertain demands of ethical requirements and, in that feeling of being overwhelmed, cannot envisage how they might introduce that uncertain position directly into their work with clients.

> How do you keep up to date with ethics that informs the work of therapists?

Preparing to implement relational ethics in action

We might assume that training programmes already equip their students with all that is required to work relationally with ethics. Of course, and as we have already acknowledged, many training courses do indeed ensure their students have a good grasp of ethics and encourage a critical engagement with top-level ethics, perhaps through the application of them drawing on therapy scenarios. As we have already outlined, however, while this is critically important, the demand of relational ethics is that we bridge that learning directly and judiciously into our work with clients; that we take *conceptual* and *theoretical* ethics and make them *relational*.

There are important steps that practitioners can take to help them position themselves to integrate relational ethics in action. We might see this as a 'chain of development' process. No one link of this chain is more important than another, and the chain is not a sequential development requirement. Like all chains, each link is an integral part of the whole and, in our move towards implementing relational ethics, we might revisit each link at different points and, indeed, revisit them at different stages. Figure 5.1 shows this in action, which we will unpack a little.

The acquisition of **theoretical and conceptual knowledge** begins, for many, through core training experiences where, as we have said, we

Figure 5.1 Ethical chain of development model

are often first introduced to the principles of ethics as they apply to therapeutic relationships. However, as we will see from different links in this chain, theoretical and conceptual knowledge will be revisited in different ways at different times. What is important, however, is that we take learning from practice, or supervision, or our continuing professional development, for example, to support our approach to ethics.

Fundamental to all our work are our **personal values and biases**, as they will shape our overarching view of the world, our experience of our working context, the clients we work with, and how we work to bridge our own experiences with those of our clients; informing our sense-making with others, while also holding them as separate and unique. As we have discussed in previous chapters, ethics sit alongside our values and biases, not only giving us a sense of our own 'rights' and 'wrongs' of the world, but also how we navigate the grey areas of ethical dilemmas.

To have insight into our own personal values and biases and, therefore, how we might make sense of situations that arise in the therapeutic process, demands an **enhanced self-awareness**. This level of self-awareness enables us to think about strengths and areas for development in our practice and theoretical and conceptual knowledge, as well as our feelings and responses to our client work and to recognise transferential and countertransferential relational processes (or how we might frame these terms within our own modality).

The use of our **skills and self** is critical in establishing, sustaining, navigating, and – ultimately – ending a therapeutic relationship that is respectful and holds the client's autonomy in focus (as well as our own self-care). Our core counselling skills are critical, including (where appropriate) the use of self-disclosure to help build trust, transparency, and a collaborative shared commitment to the relationship between client and therapist. This additionally creates the essential relational frame through which we can explore ethical issues as they arise in therapy, critically, so discussion becomes *part of the therapy* rather than sitting outside of it.

Diversity and cultural awareness are evidently critical in all our work so that we are best positioned to work alongside the diversity of the people and communities who access our services. As we discussed in Chapter 3, relational ethics arguably enables us to meet our clients in a collaborative and respectful way that holds the diversity and difference while, at the same time, facilitating a discursive bridge through which meeting points can be reached. More specifically and explicitly, if we can talk about difficulties while actively respecting each other's perspective, we hold the potential of finding ways forward while still respecting each other's position.

In the UK, supervision is a core ethical requirement of practice, as mandated as part of membership of PSA register-holding professional associations. In other territories, supervision is still held centrally to therapeutic relationships. As we know, supervision doesn't just happen, as it requires the development and holding of a relationship itself. **Configuring supervision** is about taking that process further to support the therapist's use of a relational ethics approach in their work. Specifically, we need to adopt a relational approach to ethics in our discussions in supervision about a) our client work, and b) ourselves as practitioners. Supervision supports practice, and practice informs supervision; explicitly bringing relational ethics to the table enhances both practice and supervision in a cyclical and mutually supportive way.

Finally, and equally importantly to the other links of the chain, is our **personal and professional reflexivity and development.** Within this context, we further reflect on biases and values (as discussed earlier), but also reflect on our client work and experiences. In doing so, we often revisit theoretical and conceptual ideas about practice and how they have impacted on us. We discuss these in supervision, as well as seeking out literature, books, and online resources to structure our continual professional development activities around our learning needs. In drawing on and being informed by relational ethics, we use those experiences as a reference point. As we might learn from our client work, we can also transfer that learning into our future client work; relational ethics and how we have navigated these previously – our successes and struggles – will be an important part of that.

As we have illustrated, while our core learning around ethics is critical, there is more we can do to fully engage with the relational process of ethics. We can find ways of not only bringing that explicitly into therapy dialogues, where situations arise, but also to make discussions about ethics an integral part of therapy itself. It is in this frame that we can really see the difference between top-level ethics that offer broad parameters for ethical boundaries and guidance about practice, and relational ethics that become part of therapy, supporting collaboration, mutual respect and, thus, the very relationship itself. *How* we then do this in practice is discussed below, where we offer a model for relational ethics in action.

Doing ethics relationally

Here we offer a model for doing ethics relationally in the context of helping relationships – see Figure 5.2. We offer this as a starting point, however, because consistent with how we have argued throughout,

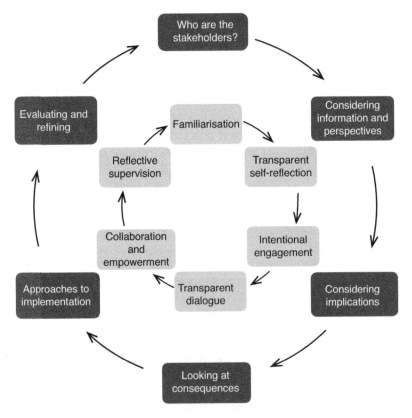

Figure 5.2 A model for relational ethics in action

this model – in this form – might not necessarily be a good fit for you. As such, we invite to you consider it and change what you need to change to make it a better fit for who you are, how you work, and the clients you work with. For example, if working with children and young people, you might think you need to adapt the language, or the focus, to best fit in such contexts.

This model represents a two-layer perspective on relational ethics, where the outer circle identifies the key considerations that can sit both within but also outside of the therapeutic relationship. This assumes that no therapy takes place in a vacuum and that decisions made within the relationship will have consequences for both the client and therapist outside of the relationship. This is a systemic perspective of therapy; that clients come to therapy and often focus on individual experiences (although this can vary depending on the cultural lens of the client), but are also part of a bigger system, which can include: family; friends; community; formal support; informal support; employment; other agencies (housing, benefits); faith, etc. In the UK, many courses have a tendency to focus solely, or primarily, on the work with the individual and, in our view, pay insufficient attention to the importance of the system.

We feel it is important to include it in this model because decisions made in therapy will almost certainly reverberate throughout the client's wider network. Our suggestion here is not necessarily that the impact on others ought to be the primary driver for ethical decision-making; rather, it needs to be part of the dialogue and *may* be an important factor in that decision-making process. Another key benefit of systemic thinking is that it can further support multidisciplinary working. Many therapists are embedded in multidisciplinary settings or draw on the skills and perspectives of others to support the client through a referral process. Being able to draw on a narrative of their collaborative ethical decision-making with a client, assuming client consent, can be hugely enabling in supporting the client with, and by, their wider system.

The inner circle of the model outlines key elements the therapist and client will need to engage with in the therapeutic process to support a relational ethical position. We will take each process in turn and offer a brief explanation, drawing on a client scenario with Shamir.

Shamir *is a 17-year-old student who is seeing a counsellor at his*
local Further Education (FE) college. It has been suggested that
he attends counselling by his tutor because she believes Shamir is
under-performing in his studies and that there may be personal
reasons for this. Shamir is uncertain about coming for counsel-
ling but did not want to disappoint his tutor. He would rather not
continue with sessions but fears that, by withdrawing, his tutor
will judge him negatively and may share concerns with his fam-
ily, who are under a great deal of financial pressure following a
redundancy.

Shamir does mention in this first session that he has been
self-injuring a little; he shows his arm to the counsellor, and some
visible cuts can be seen. He assures his counsellor this is under
his control and he has no thoughts of suicide. He is very worried
about his family and believes he would be better getting a job, to
help them out financially, because family is hugely important for
him, informed by his faith. He acknowledges that he feels high
levels of anxiety and is unhappy a lot of the time, but he thinks
his energies would be better spent job-hunting than talking with
a counsellor.

Some of the key ethical considerations here include:

How much should the counsellor persuade Shamir to engage in
  counselling, given his anxiety and self-harm?
How might others be able to support Shamir here, including his
  tutor, who is concerned for his wellbeing?
If others can be supportive, how might they be informed of
  Shamir's current position?
What are the concerns about Sharmir's self-harm – is this a safe-
  guarding concern?
Are there concerns about the potential for suicidal thoughts?
  Shamir says he has no thoughts now but a) could he be dis-
  guising these thoughts, or b) given his anxiety and concern,
  could he begin to feel more desperate?
What are the actions if Shamir does not return after this initial
  session?

Figure 5.3 Contextual considerations for relational ethics in action

Contextual considerations for relational ethics in action

Who are the stakeholders?

This is a critical first question to reflect on because, as we have already outlined, therapy never takes place in a vacuum. We can immediately identify key stakeholders in Sharmir's situation, including himself, his tutor, the college, his family, and his faith support, to begin with. We might also keep in mind the potential for future stakeholders, such as referrals we might make to formal support agencies or online support, or suggesting informal strategies for self-care. Stakeholders are those key elements of the client's system *now,* and in the *future.*

Considering information and perspectives

How stakeholders relate to each other will vary in different situations, in different contexts, and for different clients. There are some instances, perhaps in a school setting for example, where bringing stakeholders together to share information and perspectives can be critical. Likewise, what our top-level ethics tells us about managing boundaries, working with the contract, and honouring the autonomy of the client is important here too. For Shamir, he fears that if he does not attend counselling his tutor will be disappointed in him, or that it might jeopardise his studies. Whereas he also feels that he might need to withdraw from his studies to help his family and be consistent with what he imagines are the expectations of his faith. Shamir has already expressed several fears based on his assumptions of how he imagines others will see him (and is becoming immobilised in his decision-making process as a consequence). All of these considerations need gently testing out.

Considering implications

Importantly, the therapist can draw on their understanding of top-level ethics and their own experience, including around the autonomy of the client, and also how they might address any safeguarding concerns. It will be important for the therapist to talk to Shamir about these apparent competing expectations, as that will also support a discussion about Shamir's risk now, and how that might change. However, while top-level ethics will be critical, so too will be the dialogue with Shamir about his perceptions of the implications of decisions that could be made. Each possible scenario (e.g., continuing with counselling, remaining in college, leaving college to find work, keeping himself safe, etc.) needs to be teased out so that Shamir can implications-test each potential outcome.

Approaches to implementation

It is important to help clients consider decisions 'in action', to help shift thinking from the conceptual and imagined, to what it might actually look like in practice. Likewise, to help the client think about how they would implement a decision. For example, if Shamir were to decide to leave college, what would he do, who would he need to speak to (including his family) and what sort of employment might he consider (and what are the realistic prospects for that)? For the therapist, they may hold on to the importance of Shamir continuing with counselling to address his anxiety and self-harm, and to help him consider his own future. This discussion needs explicitly to attend to the way the therapist embarks upon engaging the client in this dialogue, and what the implications might be of the therapist's 'hoped-for' outcome. The implementation of decisions made may impact on the client and therapist differently and it is helpful for both (or all) parties to share these realities.

Evaluating and refining

Critically, how will each know if what is decided on is working – what will be the benchmarks that Shamir, and/or his therapist, can use to ask whether a particular decision is working or not; and if not, what actions might then be taken to refine a decision to help ethically address the changing situation? The evaluation of the discussion and any outcome can be fruitful not only in checking the validity of any decision made, but also the process by which it was achieved. This can be useful transferable learning for the client to bring to other situations in their life.

We have presented the contextual elements here in a sequential way, but the reality is this is not how it will typically be experienced. Rather, it is more likely to be a multilayered process where discussions are had within the therapeutic relationship, where different aspects of each element come into consideration. While the different elements are presented discretely here, they are unlikely to be explored one-at-a-time and, instead, will be present in a fluid and shifting way. Additionally, navigating ethics is often not a neat process and the two stakeholders in the room (client and therapist) – or more if working with couples or groups, for example – will each have different perspectives to bring. For example, with Shamir, in thinking about risk the therapist will be driven by a wish to help keep Shamir safe and to be reassured about his wellbeing; for Shamir however, he feels that it is under control and is driven more by finding a quick solution to his immediate problems. There will often be competing wishes in the process, which too need to be considered. Finally, of course, is that the model does not assume 100% consensus; there will be differences in perspectives and compromises will need to be found.

What is important here, however, is to remember that through the lens of ethics there are very few definitive 'rights' and 'wrongs', but rather different possibilities. The contextual considerations play an important part in the co-production of an ethical narrative of decision-making, which is an important reference point for good practice.

Relational ethics in the therapeutic exchange

Here we consider the inner circle of the model, which attends to the process that the therapist and clients can usefully engage with to navigate ethical issues in a relational way. See Figure 5.4, which shows relationship considerations, which we will discuss in turn.

Familiarisation

Where an ethical consideration emerges in the therapy, it is important that this is brought into the 'known'. Often, as many of us will relate to, there can be ethical decision points in the therapeutic exchange that the therapist identifies and then takes to supervision to consider solutions. While we support the active involvement of supervision in this process (and it will be discussed more fully shortly), the suggestion here is that the therapist is transparent as soon as they feel able to articulate the issue to bring the client on board. For example, the therapist could say to Shamir, '*I feel a real tension here, in that a large part of me feels that therapy could be really helpful to you with your anxiety and self-harm, but also I don't want you to feel forced to come along if you don't want to. It needs to be your decision, but I also hear how conflicted you feel too in managing these problems. I can share a sense of my own conflict here also.*'

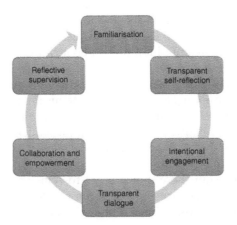

Figure 5.4 Relationship considerations for relational ethics in action

This is a valid and important therapeutic intervention, but also begins to name one of the ethical dilemmas to Shamir; indeed, the therapist could begin that sentence with '*I feel there is an ethical dilemma here for us to work through Shamir, in that a large part of me* . . . .' This validates Shamir's perspective, his autonomy in his decision-making, but also validates the dilemma the therapist is experiencing. It is introduced in a way that invites a collaborative approach to decision-making.

Transparent self-reflection

This builds on the familiarisation process, which names the area for consideration, but requires of the therapist a willingness to share their own thought processes, but in a way that does not put pressure on the client to respond in a particular way. Instead, by talking through their own thought processes the therapist is also introducing into the dialogue some possibilities for how to navigate a particular issue, which they can then begin to explore with the client more fully. Here the therapist can begin to name their inner dialogue with Shamir about the different challenges they are experiencing and perhaps, if appropriate, how that impacts on them. This models care and connection to Shamir, and may also be a moment of relational depth.

Intentional engagement

At this stage the ethical dilemma(s) will have been named (brought into the room in a transparent way) and the therapist will have begun to model different ways of thinking about working with them, including naming some feelings and thoughts about the process in terms of impact. Intentional engagement invites the client into a full and equal collaborative discussion about the different options. At this stage too, the therapist (and very possibly the client also) will be aware of the contextual factors, which we have already discussed, to help shape and inform the dialogue.

Encouraging a consideration of the stakeholders, different perspectives, implications, and consequences, this will help to encourage a collaborative intentional engagement with the ethical dilemma or decision-making process. The therapist could begin to explore with Shamir his relationship with his tutor, his education, his family, and his faith for example, as helping him to think about other key factors that might play a part in helping him, together with his therapist, work through Shamir's ambivalence about therapy. Shamir, who it seems feels out of control in his situation, may feel more respected, seen, and invited to be an equal in the exploration of his alternatives through the process of intentional engagement.

Transparent dialogue

With the ethical issue(s) identified, the therapist having been able to respond to their initial identification of those issues, modelling any thoughts or feelings that might be associated for them about the situation, and a collaborative invite offered to the client for them to work to think through how best to attend to the issues, the requirement for transparent dialogue is critical. This needs to be managed, of course, through the therapeutic modality of the therapist in how 'present' they might ordinarily see themselves in the process. However, a pluralistic position, which allows agility in the therapist to work with a client in such a way that reflects their current needs, is incredibly helpful. The transparency of the dialogue, which includes fostering trust, belief, encouragement, and empowerment, also enables both therapist and client to be fully autonomous in a mutual endeavour.

Collaboration and empowerment

This essentially is the core of relational ethics – without collaboration relational ethics simply becomes, well, unrelational. While, as therapists, we have our professional responsibilities to be mindful of, as well as the broad ethical parameters of 'top- level' ethics, the moment we look outside of the process for answers, part of us leaves the room. As if when the client is speaking, we were to look out of the window to take our inspiration from elsewhere – from outside of the relationship. In that moment, something of the relationship is, at best, stalled and, at worst, fractured. Again, this is not to say that attention to top-level ethics is not important, because surely it is. Rather, that attention to the top-level ethical requirements needs to take place *within* the relationship, and *alongside* the client.

Reflective supervision

As threads through all therapy, and has threaded through this book, supervision is a key component here. We have discussed previously the need for us to explore with our supervisors their approach to working with ethics in their practice, and in supervision, and to consider how relational ethics can be worked with in the supervisory process. It is hard to over-state how useful this is in providing a space for therapists to practise working with ethical issues relationally in a restorative and formative space, additionally considering how the 'normative' of ethics can also be attended to. We say the normative of ethics in that there will be occasions where the rights and wrongs of our actions as therapists need to be paramount, e.g., not acting on a client's attraction to us, or us to them.

Such situations need managing with care, and we would argue that a relational approach provides the most respectful space. Our task, as is always the case with supervision, is to bridge our learning from supervision back into practice, and vice versa; this is why supervision is so critical in supporting relational ethics in action. The model of relational ethics speaks to all aspects of therapy, all of the time, and is often implicitly embedded in the process. After all, there is nothing in the model outlined above that doesn't simply speak of ethical therapy across all contexts. It is the pivoting, however, from the implicit to the explicit in the discussions and considerations around ethics that makes it relational.

All these stages helpfully lead back to familiarisation, although from a slightly different perspective. This provides an opportunity to review where things are, as outcomes might include: issues being resolved; issues continuing; remaining points of difference in perspective that need to be attended to; or new issues emerging. It is important to 'close' an ethics dialogue so that therapist and client are clear about the outcome. This also informs the evaluation process, which sits as a broader contextual issue in the relational process.

Top-level and relational ethics as a continuum of thinking

As we have demonstrated in the Shamir scenario, ethical dilemmas can arise in practice all the time and don't necessarily speak to the major events we always imagine. Practitioners will often think of ethics in relation to what they experience as major, or impactful events, such as breaches of confidentiality, harm, safeguarding, breakdowns in relationships or complaints, for example. Indeed, it is true that these are major ethical considerations that need to be negotiated carefully. Our top-level ethical benchmarks can be useful in helping to frame our thinking about decisions made and a rationale for actions taken. Ethics, though, as we have discussed throughout this book, also relates to all aspects of the helping relationship that hold the balance between harm and empowerment.

Helping Shamir to think about his circumstances, whether or how he engages in therapy, the future of his education, the relationship with his family, how he makes sense of his circumstances through the lens of his faith, and his own safety as he tries to contend with what sometimes appear to be intolerable pressures for him, are all key ethical turning points too, which hold the balance of harm and empowerment in much the same way as top-level ethics. Our argument here is not that top-level ethics are not helpful and relational ethics are, but rather that they are part of the same ethical continuum. Relational ethics becomes a meaningful – and therapeutic – way of integrating ethics *into* the relationship, rather than an adjunct to it.

Chapter 6

Bringing pluralistic relational ethics to life

Case studies

Our aim in providing a pluralistic relational ethics approach in this chapter is to encourage and support practitioners to embed all aspects of ethics into their day-to-day life and ways of being. That way, it simply becomes who we are and what we do. It becomes a flexible and fluid mindset and approach. We offer three case examples compiled from people's lived and intersecting life experiences. The cases provide valuable resources for trainers, supervisors, service leads, practitioners, trainees, and anyone interested in exploring pluralistic relational ethics in action. Importantly, the case studies convey meaning-making and decision-making across a range of contexts and roles. Each case and response is presented, followed by prompts for reflection.

In engaging with the cases, in Table 6.1 below, we adapt the staged approach shown in Chapter 4 and offer you a *pluralistic relational ethics process model* to complement the models shown in Chapter 5. The model we share here is particularly helpful for more complex or challenging situations that can occur in counselling and helping work; cases where there is an evident risk or safeguarding concern. That said, it is helpful to use the model in training and supervisory contexts, to build your flexible and vigilant *response repertoire*. Like learning any new skills or ways of being, once you are familiar with the model, it will become 'second nature' and will be embedded in your work and relationships. The multistep, multidimensional model mirrors a pluralistic mindset and approach. Central to pluralistic relational ethics is deliberate practice (McLeod, 2017), which embodies the notion of careful, purposeful, systematic reflection when considering the components, features, and options in any given scenario.

When using the model, bear in mind that although it is presented in a linear fashion the components do interact and allow for creative and pragmatic ways of meaning-making and decision-making – for example through use of creative methods such as images, drawing,

DOI: 10.4324/9781003354970-6

and sand-trays. Invoking your creativity when navigating challenging situations can help you to respond reflexively to whatever situation you are facing. Experiencing and processing the situation through dialogue with colleagues or supervisors creates rich, reflexive, collaborative, and consultative decision-making.

Table 6.1 Pluralistic relational ethics: a model for ethical meaning-making and decision-making

Step	Practitioner Considerations
1	**Create a narrative:** *Capture the key people, features and context involved in the situation.* *Who and/or what does the issue or situation relate to?* *What parts are people playing in the situation?* *What relational dynamics are playing out?*
2	**Apply a pluralistic mindset to the situation:** *What ethics code, framework, or guidance is available and applicable?* *What concepts from a pluralistic approach are helpful for this situation?* *Are there issues associated with injustice, oppression, epistemic distrust?* *Work collaboratively, consult with colleagues, use shared meaning-making and decision-making.*
3	**Consider relational principles, concepts, theories:** *Identify relevant principles and concepts to inform your thinking and decisions.* *What counselling theories can you consider to support you in reflecting on and understanding the situation?*
4	**Consider support:** *Is support needed for the person or people involved in the situation?* *Do you need support, including supervision?*
5	**Identify an appropriate response:** *Consider options.* *Choose a way forward.* *Consult with relevant others to inform your meaning-making and decision-making in relation to the situation and your identified response / way forward.*
6	**Implement and reflexively review:** *Implement your chosen course of action in response to the situation.* *Evaluate your chosen course of action.* *Weave your learning back into your ongoing work and evolving way of being.*
7	**Reflect and consider the personal impact on you and on others involved:** *Identify appropriate self-care/other care.* *What learning can you draw from the event, relational situation, or issue that you can reflexively integrate into your ways of being?*

Case examples

I Abdi: second-year counsellor trainee with ethical framework concerns

Abdi is a second-year trainee counsellor. Abdi's parents were born in Kenya and came to Britain in the 1960s, to work as doctors in the NHS. Abdi was born in the 1970s and always knew that he wanted to work in mental health. Following training and working as a mental health nurse, Abdi decided to focus on counsellor training. His chosen training programme was based on a humanistic integrative approach, with trainees learning about Rogers' core conditions and the centrality of the therapist–client relationship in their first year. The second year introduced theories and concepts from the spectrum of humanistic therapies, including gestalt and transactional analysis. Abdi and fellow students were introduced to the BACP Ethical Framework (BACP, 2018) in year one of the training programme and were encouraged to use it and refer to it in both practice and supervision contexts. Abdi's understanding of ethics was that the ethical codes came into being when a practitioner encountered significant ethical challenges or crises in their therapy work. Essentially, the ethical framework was a resource to refer to when needed. For Abdi, the framework feels like an awkward, 'clunky', and inaccessible document that is somewhat remote from his day-to-day experiences and perceptions of being on a practice placement. Abdi works with a humanistic integrative supervisor, Jane, and discussion of the ethical framework does not usually feature in the supervisory meetings.

You are a trainer and consultant, engaged by a professional body consortium to work with training providers and practitioner supervisors to embed relational ethics into practitioner training programmes. Your contract with the consortium is to work with UK trainers on accredited training programmes and with accredited supervisors, to ensure that ethical fluency and literacy is a central feature of the course curriculum for all training providers and associated supervisors. In relation to the key components or features of the scenario, you know that Abdi's parents migrated to England, and that he is a first-generation member of his family to settle in Britain, intending to remain in England. There are no indications of oppression or racism in his early years and adulthood so far. Jane, Abdi's supervisor, works as a humanistic practitioner and the ethical framework is not a key feature of the supervisory work with Abdi. The training programme lead, Freda, ensures that students are introduced to the ethical framework in year one of the curriculum, using case examples to facilitate learning about responding to high risk and safeguarding situations. You can see that for Abdi, the ethical framework is an adjunct; something that stays on the shelf unless he is facing a high-risk safeguarding situation. The supervision setting is similar, with the framework only used when there are serious safeguarding concerns. Your contract with the consortium is to work with UK trainers on accredited training programmes and with accredited supervisors, to ensure that ethical fluency and literacy is a central feature of the course curriculum for all training providers and associated supervisors.

You have worked closely with the consortium and consulted with trainers, supervisors, and trainees, to inform development of training content and materials that trainers can use for their programmes. This collaborative consultative stage elicited a large amount of data to inform development of training materials and you convene a working group whose members include representation from the consortium, trainers, supervisors, trainees, and representation of client voices and perspectives. Working with the group, you build a portfolio of resources that include competency components that can be embedded in all levels of the training, along with critical theories and concepts, to be used as resources that provide alternative lenses through which to consider human change and relationships – and importantly, which challenge dominant westernised, colonised theories and practices.

Anti-oppressive practice forms the basis of all resources developed for the trainer and supervisors. You include the pluralistic relational ethics model in the concept of the *practitioner resource kits* or *toolkits* and other ethics resources (BACP, 2021; Gabriel, 2016). Abdi is involved in the working group and pilots the model with his supervisor Jane. Abdi also works with his programme tutors to pilot the resource kits, including the model. His cohort are supported to consider relational ethics in all aspects of their work and ways of being. Although this seems odd initially, Abdi and his fellow students increasingly feel more confident to congruently and authentically 'be themselves' in their therapy work. With the support of the trainers, supervisor, and peers, Abdi soon begins to understand what it means to embed ethics within himself, as a way of being and a constantly evolving mindset. Abdi loved the model, and it was soon imprinted on his mind as a flexible decision-making tool. In relation to the consortium's commission, your work is rolled out across the UK and feedback shows it is an especially popular resource with trainers and trainees, who report how much they value embedded learning about relational and interactional ways of being in therapeutic work.

Case study reflection

* How would *you* go about embedding relational ethics into practitioner training?
* What key steps would you want to put into place?
* Who would you want involved?
* How would you involve key stakeholders in the process?
* How might collaboration, consultation, and co-production feature in development of training approaches and resources?

2 David: a principled practitioner advocating 'love' in therapy

David has been in counselling and psychotherapy practice for over 30 years, both in an organisational setting in a community mental health centre that offers counselling and in his thriving private practice. As a private practitioner, David sees clients for therapy and supervises experienced practitioners. David values his professional body membership, seeing the organisation as responsible for advancing practice standards and more generally the counselling professions, and values the professional journal he receives every month as part of his membership subscription. The journal provides topical articles and general news of relevance for the counselling and mental health professions and David always looks forward to receiving his monthly copy and to engaging with the features and other content. David enthusiastically prepares and submits an article to the journal, on 'love' in the therapy setting and relationship. In the article, he provides an overview of theories and concepts associated with client–therapist phenomena related to the quality and tone of the therapy relationship including, relational depth, attunement, and attachment. He builds a case for 'love' to be part of the core relational conditions for effective client recovery and healing. When the article is published, it is greeted with a mixed reception. Some people are pleased that the topic is being openly discussed, whilst others are horrified at the prospect of love being part of their therapy work. David is surprised at some of the extremely hostile messages he receives on social media, never imagining that colleagues in the profession would be so nasty in a public domain. Over time, the toxic messages fade away and David carries on in his private practice, determined not to let the personal attacks undermine his sense of self and his confidence and competence in his work. A new private client, Alison, who works as a counsellor, starts working with David for long-term psychotherapy to work through childhood trauma. In session 5, Alison mentions that she read David's paper in the professional journal and was attracted to his take on love in therapy, and wanted to explore what this meant for their psychotherapy relationship.

How might David move forward and respond to Alison's request? In the immediate aftermath of the article being published, as he realised the impact on social media, David understands how naïve he was to imagine there would be no opposition to his thinking about love in the therapy context. He also realises how important it is to support and care for himself in the wake of the toxic hate mail and social media messages he received. He initially sought support from others, including his supervisor. Determined to carry on with deepening his understanding and exploration of love in the therapy context, David uses supervision as a supportive context in which to process his reaction to the toxic messages. He also accesses EMDR to work on the way in which the personal attacks triggered trauma responses.

In relation to working with Alison, David adopts a *deliberate practice* approach to his work. He actively and collaboratively works with Alison, sharing meaning-making and decision-making about the therapy process and content with her. He facilitates a collaborative contracting process, in which they explore key conditions and boundaries to support their work together. David shares information on how he works, sharing relevant theories and practices in relation to love in the therapy context and relationship. They discuss in detail what this might mean and agree a baseline condition that is important to David as a practitioner. Whilst David believes that love is a core condition for effective psychotherapy, he firmly believes that any sexualised acting out with a client is not OK. Alison agrees with, and is reassured by, this baseline. She wants to understand what David means by 'love' and values hearing about the theories and discussing them with David.

In their exploration of 'love', they consider gender, power, misogyny, patriarchy, and intersecting disadvantages that might impact on how experiencing empathic care and compassion and relational depth could be a discombobulating process for some – especially Alison, a woman with a history of childhood sexual abuse, and traumatic rape as a younger woman. David uses the pluralistic relational ethics model as a mental map for his work with Alison; in particular, to prompt deliberate practice, to facilitate informed, meaningful, and collaborative deliberate practice for himself and Alison, and to provide prompts for clear reflection on his work with Alison, and to remind himself that access to support and self-care is essential.

His non-defensive and open way of engaging with Alison influences the development of their good working relationship. He shares his understanding of key issues in relationships when things go wrong, including misuse and abuse of power. They explore why Alison might feel drawn to people who are abusive and oppressive. Their explorations are important for Alison. They create a rich relational and exploratory context in which Alison learns how to support and trust herself, as well as discover how to begin trusting the therapist. Over time, she becomes increasingly confident that, based on her experience with David in the therapy work and relationship, she can trust her judgement that he will not abuse her.

With David's support, and his sharing of therapy and relationship concepts drawn from humanistic and psychodynamic theories and informed by contemporary writing on power and oppression, Alison was able to explore her sexuality and sexual identity. When she initially read David's paper, she had been drawn to him without fully understanding why. It became clear to her over time that her reading and understanding of David's paper was partial and there may have been some inner destructive drive to work with someone who might ultimately be abusive towards her. Of course, David was not an abuser, and was a person who saw the value of bringing authentic and compassionate love into the therapy context and relationship.

Over time, through working collaboratively with David and through sustained in-depth exploration of her childhood trauma, Alison's trust in David deepened, and increasingly, her trust in herself deepened. Her confidence grew, and she was able to explore authentically engaging in new relationships and experiences; all the while enjoying her sense of self-respect and newfound pleasure in simply being.

Case study reflection

- How would *you* have worked with Alison?
- What issues or challenges would you encounter when working with issues associated with abuse?
- How might you explore issues associated with sex, sexual abuse, sexuality, sexual identity, sexual attraction, and arousal in the context of the therapy relationship and process?
- What is your view on 'love' in the therapy context and relationship?
- How would you use the pluralistic relational ethics decision-making model to inform the work?

3 Gabrielle: conflicted client with complex intersecting challenges

Gabrielle's great-grandparents, Joseph and Taniyah, arrived in Britain on the Empire Windrush in 1953. They settled near London, and quickly secured work in the NHS. Although Britain had invited citizens from across the British Empire to settle in mainland England, Joseph and Taniyah did not feel welcome. Across Britain in the late 1950s and 60s, it was not uncommon to see signs outside businesses and buildings that stated: '*no blacks, no dogs, no Irish*'. Such shocking and dehumanising displays had an insidious, toxic impact on Joseph, Taniyah, and their growing family. Cultural discombobulation was experienced by the family. Despite the challenges and ever-present hostility that they experienced, they settle and raise their family.

Gabrielle was born to one of Joseph and Taniyah's grandsons, Tom, who was of mixed English and African heritage. Tom had married a white middle-class lawyer, and their first child was Gabrielle. Gabrielle was light-skinned. She grew up with family stories about Jamaican and African heritages. Gabrielle was deeply disturbed by what had happened to her ancestors and felt compelled to redress her ancestors' experiences of the slave trade. Although none of her white ancestors had been involved in or benefitted from slavery, she was acutely aware of her perceived whiteness and privileged position as a well-educated member of the medical profession in the UK. Awareness of the impact of British colonisation and associated injustices formed an integral part of Gabrielle's family and upbringing. Gabrielle regularly asks herself, *what am I, who am I, am I African? Jamaican? British?* How do I reconcile my white British and black African and Jamaican heritages? Gabrielle seeks therapy to explore her identity confusion and identifies a white female counsellor, Sarah, recommended by a work colleague, and makes an appointment for an initial consultation.

What issues or challenges might Gabrielle and Sarah encounter in their work? In Sarah's practice, she offers a 45-minute free assessment session. Gabrielle and Sarah initially contract to work together for 10 sessions of counselling. Working within diversity and cross-culturally were areas of practice that Sarah was familiar with. Living and working in London, Sarah had developed a professional reputation for providing inclusive therapies. Sarah works as an integrative practitioner, drawing largely on humanistic concepts to inform her practice. She uses the pluralistic relational ethics model as a mental mind map that informs her approach to all client work.

Sarah is trained in EMDR (eye movement desensitisation and reprocessing) and DBT (dialectical behaviour therapy) and offers one-to-one counselling and group work. In her work, Sarah encourages exploration of cultural differences, working reflexively to explore heritages, to challenge injustices and oppression, and to appropriately weave these interactions and explorations into her practices and ways of being with clients. She deliberately draws on counselling research to inform her work and uses supervision as a place and process in which her knowledge and understanding of concepts and practices are constantly explored and expanded. Sarah endeavours to track her own emotional and psychological capacity to sustain herself in challenging interactions, without becoming defensive or destructive. Sarah's blend of congruence and authenticity, afforded within the boundaries of a caring and compassionate counselling relationship, provided conditions that were conducive to client engagement in the therapy relationship and work.

Gabrielle initially finds it challenging in the counselling relationship with Sarah. There was something disarming about her attentiveness and seeming care and compassion. Gabrielle soon learnt that Sarah valued inclusivity and challenged injustices. Sarah's relational spontaneity, authenticity, and warm blend of humane care and humour helped Gabrielle settle into the therapy work. She soon realised that Sarah's acceptance and positive regard were influencing her experience of the counselling and helping her to more deeply explore how she felt about her mixed-race heritage. She also valued Sarah's lovingly delivered but well- considered challenges.

Sarah challenged Gabrielle's complacency about her colour, her lack of candour with family and friends, and her feigned positive wellbeing. By session ten, Gabrielle and Sarah had developed a positive and collaborative therapy relationship. In reviewing the therapy to date, they considered the work across the ten sessions and its impact on Gabrielle. Deciding to continue beyond ten sessions, Gabrielle and Sarah agreed to work together for up to a year and identified a future way of mutually and respectfully agreeing an ending to their counselling work.

As therapy progressed, it took months for Gabrielle to feel safe enough within herself and in the therapy space, to be able to access her inner rage about racial injustices and the way her ancestors suffered through slavery. It was a deeply disturbing process of exploration, and it took a long while before Gabrielle could begin to explore these feelings and their origins. However, she trusted Sarah and gradually was able to access the terror, pain, horror, and hopelessness of her ancestor's situations.

Sarah was congruent in sharing her deep distress about how it might have been for Gabrielle's ancestors. Sarah shared her deep shame and sadness about being a privileged person living in a liberated and comfortable context, with the freedom to be – the very opposite of what Gabrielle's ancestors experienced. In one of their sessions, both Gabrielle and Sarah sobbed, recognising the futility and fragility of human life, and the horrors that humans can perpetrate. Experiencing Sarah's compassionate and caring love in the therapy space and relationship was profoundly cathartic for Gabrielle.

Case study reflection

> • How might you have worked with Gabrielle?
> • What difficulties or challenges might you have encountered?
> • How might you work with the colonial and related oppressive histories that impacted Gabrielle and generations of her family?
> • Reflect on the pluralistic relational ethics decision-making model and consider how you could use it to inform your work and relationship with Gabrielle.

Concluding comments

In this chapter, we set out a pluralistic relational ethics model for ethical decision-making and meaning-making in action. We have considered case studies and identified relational ways of navigating complex therapy processes and relationships. The following chapter pulls together key themes from the book and offers a final means by which to transition through pluralistic relational ethics.

References

BACP (2018). *Ethical Framework for the Counselling Professions.* BACP.
BACP (2021). *Good Practice in Action GPiA044: Ethical Decision-making in the Context of the Counselling Professions.* BACP.
Gabriel, L. (2016). Ethics in Pluralistic Counselling and Psychotherapy. In Cooper, M. & Dryden, W. (eds) *The Handbook of Pluralistic Counselling and Psychotherapy*, pp. 300–313. Sage.
McLeod, J. (2017). *Pluralistic Therapy: Distinctive Features.* Routledge.

Chapter 7

Integrating ethics within and across boundaries

A pluralistic prism for relational ethics

Introduction

In this final chapter, we summarise key themes from across the book and posit a pluralistic prism for relational ethics in the counselling and mental health professions.

So far, we have posited tools and models for relational ethics in action. We have provided case examples to bring ethics alive. We have had an emotive, evocative, occasionally irreverent, yet continuously compelling journey. In travelling through the book's chapters, in navigating the complex terrain of practice ethics, and whilst deeply delving into the minutiae of what happens in work with clients, we have captured rich perspectives and voices from across the counselling and mental health professions. These multiple voices, both in person, as depicted in Chapter 2, and through relevant literature, have informed our work. In this chapter, we provide key *'take away'* messages to influence and impact relational ethics, for now and for the future.

In Chapter 2 we had the true pleasure of engaging with talented pioneers of ethics in practice in the counselling professions. We discovered, through our research conversations, six significant and fundamental facts about how we can collectively rise to meet contemporary challenges through pluralistic relational ethics.

- **First,** is the centrality of training as a medium through which to learn, experiment, and push at the edges of our understanding of ourselves and our ways of being in helping relationships and beyond; essentially a quest to develop *ethical literacy.*
- **Second,** we must recognise the impact of living and relating in complex relational, social, cultural, and professional contexts that insidiously influence our ways of being.

DOI: 10.4324/9781003354970-7

- **Third**, we are obligated to recognise and acknowledge the impact and power of our personal, relational, and organisational responsibilities for how we live, breathe and manifest relational ethics in action.
- **Fourth**, we are obligated to understand, live, work, and relate in inclusive, socially just, and anti-oppressive ways; the manner of which must be informed by decolonised theories and concepts.
- **Fifth**, we must be mindful of and inform ourselves about, digitised technologies and AI, their implications for society, and consequently, for the counselling and helping professions.
- **Sixth**, we must become aware of the politics that prevail in our professions and beyond, and which influence fundamental rights for the workforce, including paid employment for counsellors and psychotherapists. Professional bodies have an important role and responsibility in relation to all six, not least as key advocates and ambassadors for both practitioners and public.

To augment each of these six areas, *positive activism* is needed to ensure that relational ethics remain contemporary and can reflexively shift across current and future generations of practitioners. The counselling and helping professions cannot be divorced from social, cultural, and political events, influences, and impacts. Our clients bring these into counselling through their lives, relationships, and associated conversations with us. Such matters are also part of what can seem like the fabric of day-to-day living, work, relationships, and life in its entirety. Hence, it is no surprise that our professional colleagues' contributions for Chapter 2 provide incisive and powerful comments on contemporary human challenges – themes reflected here.

Essential to influencing positive change and for the progression of a radical approach to relational ethics are committed, courageous, compassionate conversations that seek to ameliorate the injustices and oppression that are perniciously impacting both people and the planet. These matters find their way into our work with clients, many of whom are impacted by oppression, injustice, and climate change. Our relationships with one another and with our planet are fundamental to the future of humankind. So, without opposition to, and containment of, injustices and oppression, we cannot as a human race move forward positively and productively through the potentiality of *precarious equilibrium* (Berlin, 2013:18) – a situation in which people, communities, countries, co-exist within the context of diverse and seemingly irreconcilable difference. Whilst, at a micro level, we can influence through our work with clients, through inclusive, anti-oppressive, and compassionate therapies and mental health support, positive impacts can ripple out more widely into families, systems, and communities; essentially influencing through compassionate relational ethics. At a macro level, collectively, we can combine forces to influence social change in multiple ways; not least through burgeoning groups such as the UK group TaSC (therapy and social change), a growing network of counselling professionals and those from allied disciplines who seek to bring psychological and social concepts, alongside pragmatic compassion and action, to bear upon the urgent challenges that global communities are facing.

Precarious equilibrium is a useful concept and not one to be feared. First posited by Berlin (2013), a Russian-British philosopher, the concept offers the prospect of another way of being and behaving across communities, countries, and peoples. As a concept, it offers a heuristic prism (lens) through which to consider local, national, and global relations and factions. Precarious equilibrium also brings an underpinning organising principle and commitment to avoid destruction of self or others in the multiple processes and iterative interactions across communities and peoples. For those interested in exploring the roots of pluralism and pluralistic thinking, Berlin is worth exploring, as is William James' work on a pluralistic philosophy for human advancement, *A Pluralistic Universe* James, (1977). James was a 19th-/early 20th-century philosopher and psychologist (Araujo & Osbeck, 2023). Both James and Berlin were ahead of their time, providing concepts relevant for our contemporary complex cultural, social, and political world.

However, what Berlin and James do not offer is the 'how to' of embedding pluralism in ways relevant to the micro and macro levels of contemporary human existence. Hence, we need to quest and find routes through the hubris of day-to-day relating, working, and living and through the wider eruptions and hostilities that occur. It would be naïve and disingenuous of us to cast a future where, through a pluralistic relational ethics approach, there is no dissent. A pluralistic perspective does not get rid of dissent. What pluralism does offer is a way of being and working within complexity. We can view dissonance and disruption as the lifeblood of innovation and new discoveries; we do not need to defend against it. Essentially, what we are setting down here is a call to courageous pluralistic action.

In the following sections we briefly consider the six fundamentals identified above; all of which complement the rich research conversations in Chapter 2. Additionally, we offer critical comment and signpost horizon developments for relational ethics.

The centrality of training

Our professional bodies and regulators shape and influence practitioner training. So too do charismatic founders, expounders, and expanders of key theoretical and practice approaches. Founding characters such as Freud and Rogers profoundly influenced our professions and continue to do so. They also influence beyond the field, with psychoanalytical, psychodynamic, and person-centred theories continuing to prevail in multiple contexts including analytical critiques of politics and policies, plus the influence of Rogerian informed concepts within community mental health transformation in the UK. There is, however, a paucity of research and writing on counsellor training. In 1994, Mary Connor (1994) offered a comprehensive unsurpassed template for practitioner training. However, in contemporary climes, little exists to capture the pragmatic needs of today's practitioners.

Fortunately, there is a growing body of therapy-related literature which questions the dominance of westernised and colonial influences and holds value for those involved in delivering practitioner training. Questioning the individualised and autonomous interpretation of human identity, with reference to counsellors in training, Shanee Barraclough (2023) posits alternative notions of practitioner identity. In that process, Barraclough introduces ways of working that recognise diverse cultures and perspectives (Barraclough, 2023), and form a post-human interpretation of being and relating across diverse peoples. As Barraclough (2023) notes:

> As counsellors, through such a posthuman attention, we can pursue a shared aim of participating in, ethically and responsibly, the reconfiguring of the...unsettling and remaking [of] boundaries and of opening up possibilities for multiple different ways of knowing, being and becoming counsellor.

Barraclough (2023) posits that it is our *response-ability* to respond to injustices (our own and others); a commitment that is ever-present and never ending. This turn to a post-human perspective has been increasingly evident in recent perspectives papers and in the growth of social change groups in the counselling and psychology fields. It is time to consider these philosophical shifts, and associated relational and behavioural changes, in the context of practitioner education. From our conversations with contributors (Chapter 2), we know that teaching and learning about relational ethics and understanding the complexity of how we navigate day-to-day ethics and consider issues such as relational power and oppression is lacking in training. There were concerns about the importance of teaching and engaging trainee practitioners with key constructs of importance to relational ethics, including: how to be with self and others, building self-understanding and reflexivity, and learning about how to interact with other people. Training should be less about multiple theories and concepts, and more about the self of the practitioner and self in relationship with others. It needs to consider how they are in relationship, what they understand about things like decolonisation, relational power, oppression, compassion, congruence, authentic relating, social injustices, and anti-oppressive practices.

Teaching about ethics needs to truly engage people: to bring content, material, and conceptualisations about ethics into some kind of enlivened context where people can fully grasp it. Chapter 2 contributors identified the need for people to learn how to be alongside someone who despairs about being in the word. As Rich conveyed during a research conversation that underpins Chapter 2, learning about important relational things like that precious gift of 'you can talk' and enabling the client to bring their despair into therapy work, rather than have the therapist rush to get the ambulance, or the meds, or whatever else, is fundamental. There is something important about liberating the therapy space and accompanying the client as they work and walk through their despair and distress. And you sit alongside them, with their despair. Training needs to be the key context in which practitioners learn about these things, about their *response-ability* and how to nurture their approach to relational ethics. In one of our case scenarios in Chapter 6, we posed a situation where a professional body consortium commissioned training materials for facilitating learning about ethics and how to embed them in practice. This is one way in which professional bodies could support practitioners and trainers to innovate their ethics toolkits and bring them into a contemporary landscape.

Living and working in complex systems

The relational, social, cultural, and professional contexts that insidiously influence our ways of being, actually form the fabric of our cultures, communities, and societies. Hopefully humane in nature, they shape who we are, what we do, and how we do things; they make us the change agents we become as counselling and mental health professionals. However, the shadow side of complex systems and societal roles can be toxic and pernicious being and behaving. Sadly, these unsavoury aspects of humanity are everywhere, even within the counselling and helping professions. We cannot claim to be exclusively sound, reasonable, and compassionate people or systems, or therapy organisations, or bodies that represent helping professions. We too, are forever flawed. That does not mean we cannot manage and mediate our destructive forces; we can, and we can do this constructively, collaboratively, and creatively.

Erving Goffman (2022) offers a fascinating sociological perspective on complex societal and system interactions. Undoubtedly, relationships between people, but also within systems and organisations are convoluted and dynamic. Psychodynamic concepts can offer a helpful lens through which to view the ethics of these multifaceted interactions and relationships. The emotional and psychological power of organisations and systems is addressed well in Obholzer and Roberts' (2019) edited volume on the unconscious at work. Significantly, the endeavour needs practitioners who can recognise, acknowledge, accept, and actively address their pathologies and peculiarities, in the spirit of progressive practice. Arguably, such work and ways of being demand constant vigilance, with concomitant recognition that at times, we must step aside from inevitable system and relational stresses to simply *be.*

Impact, power, and responsibilities

As counselling and mental health professionals, we are obligated to recognise and acknowledge the impact and power of our personal, relational, and organisational responsibilities for how we choose to live, breathe, and manifest relational ethics in action. Of course, it would be disingenuous to imply that we have full agency and choice. We do not. We live and work in systems, in communities, in political regimes, and hence our choices are both relationally and contextually limited.

Practice ethics within the counselling and helping professions have been heavily influenced by medical ethics (Beauchamp and Childress, 2019) which embed the notion of the benevolent expert practitioner. Beauchamp and Childress (2019) provide valuable material for work within biomedical ethics and their exemplar text is now in its eighth edition. However, their work is largely rooted in a westernised and medicalised approach and the relational, cultural, social, and political aspects of ethics in practice are underexplored; hence our offer here, and the invitation to cast a pluralistic lens on relational ethics.

Within the context of the counselling professions, Gillian Proctor's textbooks (2014; 2017) offer excellent critiques and sobering reminders of the centrality and complexity of relational power. More recently, Laura Winter and Divine Charura (2023) published their *Handbook of Social Justice in Psychological Therapies: Power, Politics, Change*, which offers a multidisciplinary, multidimensional collection of excellent resources for those seeking to challenge injustices and provide rich resource material for practitioners. Whether we are considering power and responsibility from an individual practitioner perspective, or from another role within the profession, such as trainer, or supervisor, or employer, our relational ethics apply and must be embedded in our meaning making, decision-making and actions. Whether we are revising and updating a training programme to better reflect key areas like inclusivity, decolonisation, and anti-oppression, or learning more about being a supervisor in a complex helping landscape, we must elicit our humility, courage, creativity, and compassion, to devise humane and compassionate ways forward.

Inclusive, decolonised professions

We are incontrovertible in our obligations to understand, live, work, and relate in inclusive, socially just, and decolonising ways. However, we must quest and chart decolonised ways forward, we cannot presume that westernised or European therapies and theories apply globally. Such arrogance no longer has a place in the helping professions. We must view existing exemplars through a decolonising lens as well as review their content for other injustices, exclusions, or misdemeanours. It is no longer ok to say, 'that was then', because 'this is now' and we urgently need critical curiosity to foster inclusive thinking, behaving, and being. This is not a time for complacency. To help us find ways forward there are a growing number of texts. These include recent books from Dwight Turner (2021; 2023), who offers an incisive and compelling approach to the impact of colonisation and ways forward in relation to decolonisation. Additionally, Myira Khan (2023) provides a comprehensive and insightful anti-oppressive approach to working within diversity. Khan distinguishes between 'working with' and 'working within'. The former concept holds anti-oppressive mindsets and approaches as external, whilst the latter conveys the absolute importance of deeply and authentically embedding inclusive attitudes and anti-oppressive ways of working and being within our practice, relationships, and life.

Dwight Turner's (2021; 2023) texts on colonisation and supremacy provide a compelling account of the impact of abuse of power and responsibility through patriarchy, colonialism, and misogyny. Turner (2021; 2023) and others (see Winter and Charura, 2023) also consider intersecting disadvantages and injustices. Additionally, Laura Winter and Divine Charura's (2023) handbook provides a veritable cornucopia for considering social justice within the counselling professions.

As fast as authors generate new works, interest in the need to go beyond decolonisation, towards critical theories and practices, continues to rapidly grow. More authors are calling for social transformation, rather than cultural and social accommodation or incorporation (Barham, 2023; Ghaddar and Caswell, 2019). This call to action signifies a curious intellectual precipice for anti-oppressive thinking, practice, and social action. Whilst Ghaddar and Caswell focus on Indigenous peoples, going beyond decolonisation takes us into terrain where we must acknowledge human diversity and associated injustices and oppression (Khan, 2023), and identify ways of co-existing across cultural, social, and geographical distances, in compassionate and humane ways.

It is incumbent upon trainers, trainees, trained practitioners, supervisors, and everyone involved in the delivery of the counselling professions, to be up to date on developments in theory and practice, as well as actively engaged in making positive change to challenge and extinguish oppression and the othering of people and cultures who are simply different by virtue of their age, race, gender, class, sexuality, religion, or any other dimension of difference. Whilst humans can be kind (humankind), they can also be inhumane. It is time to positively move forward and address oppression, injustice, and exclusion, both within and outside of the counselling and helping professions.

Power and potentiality of digitisation and AI

We can never rest on our laurels in relation to digitisation and AI. We must be vigilant, keep abreast of advances, and consider how ongoing innovations in AI may influence work in the counselling and helping professions. Importantly we need evidence, evaluation, and research into the values and virtues of digitised apps and AI. Whilst we may be a long way from a future in which humanoids deliver therapy and mental health work, it is likely to happen. Some post-human visions would have us consider a dystopian earth where humanoids rule. Whatever our thoughts on melding human and artificial intelligence, we cannot ignore rapid AI developments that will inevitably impact the counselling and mental health professions. So far, there are limited texts on the future of digitisation and AI in relation to helping professions. Terry Hanley, a key player in the UK in relation to tracking AI advances and considering the impact of digitisation, urges us to keep abreast of developments (Hanley, 2021). Hanley also emphasises that counselling professions must be ethically sensitive to the impact and implications of new technologies for the counselling professions. By implication, professional bodies must be key players in exploring the ethical and professional implications of AI.

Political and relational powerplays

As a major mental health workforce, we must be mindful of the politics (with both a small and a large 'p') that prevail in the counselling and mental health professions and beyond, which influence fundamental rights for practitioners. Organisations that employ mental health practitioners must address unjust inequities, including cases of low wages. This can be done in positive and productive ways to secure quality employment for counselling and helping professionals.

It is, however, incumbent upon us to identify ways of collaborating across professions, organisations, and political parties to gain better understanding and clarity about emerging mental health needs of our nations and the roles available and required to address those needs. Remarkably, there are politicians in political parties in the UK who do not understand what counselling is or grasp the fact that there is a sizeable and well-trained mental health workforce available through the body of counsellors and psychotherapists. Nor do they fully realise how therapy can help people to improve their sense of mental wellness.

Progression necessitates positive radical action. A radical approach reaches into the root causes of phenomena. Of prime significance is an openness to transparency, and to challenging oppression and domination (Ghaddar and Caswell, 2019). Within the UK there are several counselling and psychology groups and networks who are seeking to influence positive social action, including the Therapy and Social Change Network, the Pluralistic Network, Therapists Connect, and Counsellors Together UK. Psychologist Mick Cooper (2023) recently offered a rich narrative and vision for change through his publication *Psychology at the Heart of Social Change: Developing a Progressive Vision for Society* and there are increasing numbers of practitioners seeking to support progressive professional and societal change that is inclusive and socially just.

At the core of positive change is the need to hold our nerve, confront defensive internalised or external silencing, and elicit our courageous selves to influence progression. As a reader, you might ask, why? Well, counsellors and mental health professionals provide invaluable, whilst relatively hidden, support for people struggling with their mental health and wellbeing. Practitioners are well trained and able to work with complex human issues, including severe and enduring mental ill-health. Practitioners are chameleon-like and can enhance or adapt core practice skills and knowledge to provide a range of valuable mental health interventions. For example, dyadic therapy, group work, and combination therapies such as 'walk and talk', through CPD opportunities, can be provided as part of a practitioner's core knowledge and skills set. However, unless the multitalented nature of the counselling professions is promoted, evidenced, and valued, its practitioners remain under-utilised mental health resources. Activist groups and professional bodies have much work to do, to raise the profile of the counselling professions and to increase recognition of their impact.

A pluralistic prism for relational ethics

Evolving through the pages of this book has been the concept of a pluralistic relational ethic. Here, we extend that concept by introducing the notion of a *pluralistic prism* for relational ethics. The prism forms an anchor for complex ideas associated with ethics in action. Often a hexagonal shape, the multiple faces of the prism capture images and text – see Figure 7.1. As an entity or artefact, a prism is not a new idea.

Figure 7.1 A pluralistic prism for relational ethics

What is new, however, is the way we are repurposing the prism for the benefit of a pluralistic relational ethic.

Prisms were a key feature of the ancient Assyrian people; an advanced civilisation who were ahead of their time and were considered pioneers of many foundational systems that underpin the contemporary world. Often in the form of a large hexagonal shaped tall stone, the creators used the ancient Assyrian cuneiform to depict and narrate their stories, setting down important features of their race and culture. The Assyrians used prisms to record their achievements and to denote the capture of lands and other peoples. Juxtapose that prism with 21st-century navigation of ethics and we have a form of containment that can capture the multifaceted aspects of our practice. These are detailed on each of its angles, showing knowledge, models, tools, and vignettes, to inform our day-to-day navigation of relational ethics.

For our purposes here, we use the prism as a metaphorical and heuristic device to capture the multiple and complex components of everyday relational ethics and ways of being. When using the prism, we are aiming for an approximation to *precarious equilibrium* (Berlin, 2013: 18). Essentially, this is a place of recognition and constant relational vigilance. A place within which we acknowledge the uncomfortable coexistence of multiple complexities, expectations, and theoretical preferences.

We invite you to consider the prism as a means through which to engage in a constant comparison and vigilance within your practice. The ancient interpretation offered people a lasting means through which to identify and reflect upon the actions and achievements of a community or society. We offer the prism as a creative means through which to consider your practice, with each facet of the prism a lens through which you can capture the fine-grained detail of your approach to relational ethics. See it as a creative *way-marker* to signpost and chart the minutiae of therapy life and living; it provides a means through which you can present your work within a range of professional or supervisory contexts.

Navigating ethics in action demands personal and relational shapeshifting in our ways of thinking, being, and behaving. The spirit and act of questing for ethical encounters and of being a courageous presence, form central tenets of pluralistic relational ethics. These ways of being are unique to and nuanced through individuals, pairings/dyads, as well as within the contexts of groups and diverse cultures. The stuff of madness juxtaposed with exhilarating inspiration – that can be the experience of coexisting simplicity and complexity within any given meaning-making or decision-making moment. It is both sobering and stirring. It is no mean feat being a counselling and mental health professional. However, applying a pluralistic relational ethic provides fluidity and demands reflexivity to facilitate never-ending growth, learning, and development.

Concluding comments

We have quested and charted innovative ways of being and relating with self and others. We have offered you a range of process models, from which you can select those that work for you. We have advocated a pluralistic relational ethic that provides a dialectical and discursive process. Relational ethics depicts a way of being on an ethical journey co-created by client and therapist. Here 'client' and 'therapist' refer to a range of possible roles within the counselling and mental health professions. We believe that what is fundamental are the principles of collaboration and commitment to inclusive inquiry. With the aid of our collaborator colleagues who contributed to Chapter 2, we have set down iterative and positive ways forward for a pluralistic relational ethic. The call to action here is to prise open received wisdom and question a biased focus or rooting of perspectives within a western-ised philosophical or cultural tradition. The counselling and helping professions must ensure exemplars and concepts are fit for purpose for contemporary relational ethics, and for the multicultural and diverse people, communities, and societies that exist. Importantly, there is a powerful contemporary activist element growing in the helping pro-fessions; it remains to be seen whether and how this influences positive societal change.

So, we have charted a multidimensional multiverse of relationships, contexts, and interactions. We acknowledge and accept that an inten-tionally diverse approach to relational ethics demands an eternal and vigilantly nuanced approach to navigating our day-to-day working and relating. Our ethical encounters become our myriad lived lives, relationships, and work experiences. *We are ethics.*

Postscript reflection

- Consider this. It's 2090.
- What approach to relational ethics is needed in a scenario where we have humanoids that look like me, you, us?
- How do we navigate morals, meaning-making, and decision-making in a human-humanoid world?
- What does this prospect of coexisting humans and humanoids evoke for you?
- What are the implications for counselling and mental health professions?
- As counselling and helping professionals, what do we need to do to prepare for such a scenario?

References

Araujo, Saulo de Freitas & Osbeck, L.M. (2023). *Ever Not Quite. Pluralism(s) in William James and Contemporary Psychology.* Cambridge University Press.

Barham, P. (2023). *Outrageous Reason: Madness & Race in Britain & Empire, 1780–2020.* PCCS Books.

Barraclough, S. (2023). On Becoming a Counsellor: A Posthuman Reconfiguring of Identity Formation for Counsellors-in-training. *British Journal of Guidance & Counselling.* doi:10.1080/03069885.2023.2172550

Beauchamp, T.L. & Childress, J.F. (2019). *Principles of Biomedical Ethics.* Oxford University Press.

Berlin, I. (2013). *The Crooked Timber of Humanity.* Fontana.

CDLI Literary 000371, ex. 006 artifact entry (No. P384786). (2023, June 15). Cuneiform Digital Library Initiative (CDLI). https://cdli.ucla.edu/P384786 (Original work published 2008)

Connor, M. (1994). *Training the Counsellor: An Integrative Model.* Routledge.

Cooper, M. (2023). *Psychology at the Heart of Social Change: Developing a Progressive Vision for Society.* Polity Press.

Ghaddar, J.J. & Caswell, M. (2019). 'To Go Beyond': Towards a Decolonial Archival Praxis. *Archival Science.* 19, 71–85. doi:10.1007/s10502-019-09311-1

Goffman, E. (2022). *The Presentation of Self in Everyday Life.* Penguin Modern Classics. Penguin Books.

Hanley, T. (2021). Researching Online Counselling and Psychotherapy: The Past, the Present and the Future. *Counselling & Psychotherapy Research.* doi:10.1002/capr.12385

James, W. (1977). *A Pluralistic Universe.* Harvard University Press.

Khan, M. (2023). *Working within Diversity: A Reflective Guide to Anti-Oppressive Practice in Counselling and Therapy.* Jessica Kingsley Publishers.

Obholzer, A. & Roberts, V.Z. (2019). *The Unconscious at Work.* 2nd edn. Routledge.

Proctor, G. (2014). *Values and Ethics in Counselling and Psychotherapy.* Sage.

Proctor, G. (2017). *The Dynamics of Power in the Counselling and Psychotherapy. Ethics, Politics and Practice.* PCCS Books.

Turner, D. (2021). *Intersections of Privilege and Otherness in Counselling and Psychotherapy: Mockingbird.* Routledge.

Turner, D. (2023). *The Psychology of Supremacy: Imperium.* Routledge.

Winter, L.A. & Charura, D. (2023). *The Handbook of Social Justice in Psychological Therapies: Power, Politics, Change.* Sage.

Author biographies

Series editors and textbook authors

Lynne Gabriel is an award-winning Professor of Counselling & Mental Health, based at York St John University, where she is founder-director of the University's Communities Centre. Lynne is passionate about ethics and has written two textbooks on ethics in counselling and psychotherapy. Lynne also works as an ethics consultant. Lynne is active in the mental health field and has a lead partnership role in the City of York's community mental health transformation. In 2023, Lynne was appointed as BACP President.

Andrew Reeves is a Professor in Counselling Professions and Mental Health at the University of Chester, a BACP Senior Accredited Counsellor/Psychotherapist, an EMCC Senior Accredited Coach and Coach Supervisor, and a Registered Social Worker. He has worked as a practitioner for nearly 40 years in a full range of working settings, including child protection, adult mental health crisis intervention, the charity sector as well as in schools and universities. His research area is working with risk in the helping professions and he has published widely in this area.

Co-authors of Chapter 2

Peter Blundell is Senior Lecturer in Counselling and Psychotherapy Practice at Liverpool John Moores University. Peter is a social worker and a person-centred/experiential therapist. Peter's research and teaching interests include boundaries in professional practice, harm in therapy, power, and anti-oppressive practice. He is often found on social media discussing all these topics (@drpeterblundell).

Myira Khan is a multi-award-winning Accredited Counsellor, Supervisor, Coach, Trainer, Founder of the Muslim Counsellor and Psychotherapist Network (MCAPN) and author of *Working Within Diversity – A Reflective Guide to Anti-oppressive Practice in Counselling and Therapy.*

Rich Knight (he/they) is a Counsellor, Supervisor and DBT therapist with complex life limiting physical / cognitive and Neurodivergent disabilities. He is proud to cross many intersections of Race, Gender, and Class. His PhD research looks at the client experience of working with him through pluralistic collaborative and productive means to improve his clinical practice and that of the profession. Passionate about lived experience, ethics and clinical practice.

Gillian Proctor is a lecturer and research fellow at the University of Leeds and an independent clinical psychologist. She is passionate about ethics, politics and practice in person-centred psychotherapy and has written several books and numerous book chapters and articles on associated subjects.

Dwight Turner is Course Leader on the Humanistic Counselling and Psychotherapy Course at the University of Brighton, a PhD Supervisor at their Doctoral College, a psychotherapist and supervisor in private practice. His publications include *The Psychology of Supremacy (2023)*, and *Intersections of Privilege and Otherness in Counselling and Psychotherapy (2021)*, which are both published by Routledge, together with several chapters in anthologies on aspects of counselling and psychotherapy, and over 50 academic papers on everything from intersectionality in psychotherapy, to dreamwork, to Afrocentric spirituality.

A leading driver in Intersectional Psychotherapy, Dr Turner is an experienced conference speaker, including numerous keynote presentations. Dr Turner has also run workshops for a wide variety of universities, charities, and private organisations on issues of race, difference and intersectionality in counselling and psychotherapy. Dr Turner can be contacted via his website www.dwightturner-counselling.co.uk and can be followed on social media on LinkedIn, Threads, or on Twitter at @dturner300.

Hadyn Williams is an integrative psychotherapist who was CEO of BACP from 2015 to 2022. He has worked within many contexts in which counselling and psychotherapy have purpose, both as a practitioner and also as a manager of large and diverse services. Currently, he is an independent executive consultant and coach supporting senior managers within the corporate and not-for-profit sectors.

John Wilson is an international bereavement specialist whose books on grief and loss have been bestsellers – most recently *The Plain Guide to Grief* (2020). Dr Wilson delivers bereavement counselling in the UK, in person, and in partnership with Onlinevents.co.uk, provides grief workshops and practitioner training that attracts international delegates.

Index

For Product Safety Concerns and Information please contact our EU
representative GPSR@taylorandfrancis.com Taylor & Francis Verlag GmbH,
Kaufingerstraße 24, 80331 München, Germany

Printed and bound by CPI Group (UK) Ltd, Croydon, CR0 4YY
08/06/2025
01897005-0001